BALKANIZED AT SUNRISE

How a Sci-Fi Author Was Recruited to Keep a
President from a War Crimes Indictment

By Joe Tripician

PRINTED IN THE UNITED STATES OF AMERICA

BALKANIZED AT SUNRISE

How a Sci-Fi Author Was Recruited to Keep a President from a War Crimes Indictment

All Rights Reserved.

Copyright © 2010 Joseph Tripician

Revised April 2016

ISBN: 978-0-557-49451-4

Table of Contents

MAIN CAST OF CHARACTERS v

1. "Early Riser" 1

2. "Good Morning, Paranoia" 12

3. "Back to School" 25

4. "Diplomatic Ignominy" 27

5. "Bloody History" 33

6. "Today We Have Lunch at the Mass Graves" 39

7. "In Tito's Shadow" 49

8. "Some of My Best Friends Are War Criminals" 53

9. "The Smoking Guns" 56

10. "Enemy of the State" 59

11. "Bombs Can't Stop the Drink" 63

12. "War, What War?" 69

13. "War Crimes and Miss Demeanors" 72

14. "And the Winner Is" 77

15. "Home Is Where They Shave" 89

16. "A Yellow Farewell" 94

17. "Balkan Hangover" 99

18. "How Do I Put This in My Resume?" 102

ADDENDUM 1 "What Could Go Wrong?" 109

ADDENDUM 2 "Love Letter from Miles" 113

ADDENDUM 3 "AKA Eddie Bell" 119

ADDENDUM 4 "Biting My Tongue" 121

About the Author 125

MAIN CAST OF CHARACTERS

JOE TRIPICIAN: Recently divorced writer-producer, resident of New York City

DOCTOR TONY: Joe and Jakov's doctor

JAKOV SEDLAR: Film Director, Cultural Attaché of the Republic of Croatia to the US

MARTIN SHEEN: American actor

GEORGE RUDMAN: Researcher, former translator for the Bosnian Croats

ROMAN LATKOVIC: Journalist, resident of New Jersey, granted political asylum in the US

IVO SKORIC: Peace activist, NYC resident, granted political asylum in the US

MATE BOBAN ("The Mobster"): President of the Bosnian Croats

JADRANKA: Resident of Zagreb, Croatia

DOUGLAS DAVIDSON: Information Officer, American Embassy to Croatia

PETER GALBRAITH: Former US Ambassador to Croatia

RICHARD HOLBROOKE: Former US Assistant Secretary of State

"THE PRIEST": Member of the Bosnian Croat Federation, close advisor to Mate Boban

DAMIR: Operator of the only opposition radio station in Zagreb

AIDA: Translator, resident of Sarajevo, Bosnia-Herzegovina

MILES RAGUZ: former "advisor" to the Bosnian Muslims / Bosnian Croats

THE LEADERS, circa 1997

FRANJO TUDJMAN: President of Croatia

SLOBODAN MILOSEVIC: President of Serbia

ALIJA IZETBEGOVIC: President of the Presidency of Bosnia-Herzegovina

Chapter One

"Early Riser"

"Whatever it is, I'm against it."
– Groucho Marx

One glorious summer night in New York, I'm at a backyard barbeque. The air is filled with the smell of hotdogs and vodka.

I look across the yard and see her. She's a cute blonde, with a great laugh. And she's a former adult film actress.

I walk over and offer her a drink. "It's a beautiful night for a Bar-B-Q, isn't it? Yeah, I'll miss the city. Tomorrow I fly to Bosnia. It's a little colder there. Be gone, I don't know how long …" Pause for dramatic effect. "How's your drink?"

At first she smiles. Then a small furrow creases her brow. It only makes her cuter. "Bosnia? But isn't that a war zone?"

"I'm on a journalistic assignment. Cover the Balkans: bullets, bombs, war criminals … Don't know if I'll come back … Do you live nearby?"

Her smile returns. "Just down the block."

"Well, then: let's go!"

"Oh, you brat!" She laughs at my shameless attempt.

Shameless, perhaps – but by the night's end, definitely successful.

* * *

I've been waiting all my life for a pick-up line like that. It was the summer of '97 when it fell into my lap – the way things have done all my life. Now, I'm not a guy who likes to get wrapped up in politics, but I always had a fascination with strange lands and strange people. As a kid, I'd huddle under the covers and read science fiction all night.

During the day everyone I'd pass was either a good alien or a bad alien; and it was my job to identify the bad ones.

But in '97 it was my recent divorce and massive debt that started my real-life adventure.

* * *

He wears pinky rings and a yearlong tan. A proud Italian American, he lives in Long Island, and buddies with the local Mob there. He is my doctor, and he is about to make an introduction that will send me to the former Yugoslavia on a semi-clandestine job.

"Joe," begins Doctor Tony, "come into my office. We gotta talk."

The IV has barely left my arm, and I struggle to hold the cotton swab firmly in place.

"Just keep pressing down on it, and come in." Doc is rushing today. He must have just had a conversation with his mechanic – or his ex. "You still doing film, right?"

"Right."

"Well, I got a job for ya … His name is Jakov." Pronounced: "YACK-off!"

Jakov Sedlar was then Croatia's cultural attaché, the country's most famous theatre and film director, and the official media point man for the government. He'd made a film about a Croatian priest, Archbishop Stepinac, who had a reputation as a quisling for the Croatian terrorist gang called the Ustasha during WWII. Under the protection of Fascist Italy and Nazi Germany, the Ustasha ordered the forced conversion of Orthodox Serbs to Catholicism, and deported nearly 120,000 Serbs to Serbia. Their policy towards these Orthodox Serbs was "convert a third, expel a third, and kill a third." Jakov attempted to repudiate Stepinac's compliance with the Ustasha through Schindler-like testimonials of those Jews whose lives he'd saved. To this day, the very mention of the name Stepinac can separate a room filled with otherwise party-loving Serbs and Croats.

Jakov also made a film called *Gospa*, starring Martin Sheen. It depicted the "miracle" of the Virgin Mary appearing to school kids in a small town in Herzegovina, (the land separating Bosnia proper from the Adriatic). A convenient miracle, according to some: the local Croatian Franciscans needed a miracle to save their parishes from being taken over by the diocesan church.

Jakov's films reflected the patriotic nationalistic yearnings of a newly democratized Eastern European country. As art, his films were flat; as propaganda they were obvious. They were workmanlike, but not inspired or inspiring, as true propaganda should be. It was no wonder he was the Minister of Culture.

Within Croatian cultural circles Jakov had earned the moniker "The Leni Riefenstahl of Croatia." Privately, I added: "but without the talent."

I knew none of this when I first met Jakov. I couldn't have found Croatia on a map, but I had to find some income before I went bankrupt.

My production company was hurting, the result of my divorce two years previously. My ex-wife had also been my business partner. When we broke up, I bought out her half of our small company. In an effort to keep my business and myself afloat, I had accumulated over $50,000 in credit card debt. Most went into video equipment that quickly became obsolete with the rapid advancements in digital technology.

In '92 I won an EMMY award for a documentary I produced and co-directed ("Metaphoria"). But in '97 that statue collecting dust on the shelf was not bringing in paying work.

My cards were maxed, my income was falling, and I had resorted to crashing art openings for the free finger food that was my daily dinner. I was 43 years old, and one bus ride away from moving back in with my parents. So when a job came by that looked too good to be true, I took it.

Jakov's massive frame is large, as is his toothy smile, yet he moves with the agile urgency native to one used to giving and following orders. He hires me to produce an animated map of Croatia for a travelogue he's directing. He brings in a pile of brochures on Croatia: the seashore, the mountains, the industry, the nightlife – everything but a map.

Then he tosses me another brochure with a photo of Bill Clinton shaking hands with a white-haired man named Franjo Tudjman, and says: "Here is your president and our president." He smiles proudly, endearingly, paternally. "Clinton loves Croatia."

Nowhere is there a mention of the war that ended in '95. And there is no map. So, I head over to the Rand McNally store and get the only map of the Balkans they have.

It has a big disclaimer on it: "Sizes subject to change from acts of war."

Jakov also wants help with the English narration script. I start by offering advice on the title. Jakov's first choice, *Croatia: Land of 1,100 Islands & 101 Dalmatians,* doesn't quite have the zip of a blockbuster. I suggest: *Croatia: Small Country, Big Fun.* For several minutes he seriously considers it.

Jakov also needs help on the script for a second film he's making: a biography of the President of Croatia – this man Franjo Tudjman, "Clinton's friend." Being as ignorant as the next American on the subject, I look over the script for grammar, sentence structure, and the peculiar cultural attitudes and biases which make the script at times as awkward as a hippo on stilts. Then there is the Jewish question.

"I think this part of the script here …" I point. He peers at the script. "This will be particularly sensitive," I say. "Especially if you plan to screen this film in New York."

The script describes, with scanty details, the controversy surrounding Tudjman's book, *The Horrors of War,* in which he claims that the Jews helped run the most notorious Nazi death camp in Croatia – Jasenovac, or "Croatian Auschwitz," as it was known.

"Yes, yes …" he nods, somewhat distracted, knitting his large brows. I don't know if he is agreeing with me, disagreeing with me, or just doesn't get my point.

"You understand? It's a sensitive issue in New York. There's a large Jewish community here."

Jakov nods. He understands. But I don't understand much about Jasenovac …

I give Jakov my notes, and don't see him again for another couple of months.

* * *

At my next appointment with Doctor Tony, I ask him how he got hooked up with this guy Jakov.

"Oh," says Tony, as if trying to remember what he had for dinner last month, "through some broad I was banging."

"Well, Doc, anyway, I have to thank you for getting me this gig."

Tony smiles slyly: "I told Jakov: 'Joe's the best guy for the job, so don't fuck him over.'"

"That was awfully nice of you."

"Now, Joe, I want ya to speak to my pal Lenny. He owns a string of restaurants on the island, and his son wants to get into show business…"

* * *

When Jakov completes his film, he hands me a copy and tells me it has premiered in LA.

I screen the film. Martin Sheen is the narrator. In the opening credits I see: "Directed by Jakov Sedlar – and Joe Tripician."

Now, I don't often mind sharing a directing credit, but I usually prefer to have actually worked on the film. At this point, my production assistant Erin, a devilish mind in a pixyish body, starts referring to Jakov as my "Croatian sugar daddy."

One day, about six in the morning, my cell phone rings. I stumble out of a girlfriend's bed and fumble for it.

"Hello, Joe, this is Jakov!"

"Oh, hi." I try to sound cheery, but it comes out as a growl. I am definitely not ready for this call. "Where are you?"

"I am in Zagreb!" I wonder what this call was costing me. "Sorry, Joe, but please – we need you to videotape a message to our president.

"*Who* do you want me to tape?"

"Oh, no. It's just you. Just you saying few words about President Tudjman – three or five minutes. And you can do today on tape. And I have car pick it up at noon."

"Wait – what, where— ? I don't know what you're talking about, Jakov. You want me to say something into the camera? I don't know anything about Tudjman."

"Oh, no, don't to worry. I fax you script."

I rush back to my office and grab the fax: "Franjo Tudjman is a very interesting and controversial person … He established new democratic country after thousand years … Tudjman is really Croatian George Washington—"

It's a little over the top, perhaps, but I can play with it.

So, I put on my only suit, set up the lights, the camera, and ask Erin shoot it for me.

Erin gives me the signal: "Croatian Sugar Daddy – Take One!"

"Erin, stop saying that!" I'm staring at the camera. "Erin, stop laughing!"

I begin blathering into the lens, feeling I must be doing something very wrong, but not exactly sure what.

"Tudjman is a man who has been called the George Washington of his beloved country …"

One day, I know, this is going to come back to haunt me.

* * *

Wouldn't you know, a few weeks later, Jakov calls again.

"Joe, I have new job for you. A very big project, very important book: the biography of Franjo Tudjman. You will write book."

"What?" I blurt.

"Yes. I want you to write official biography of Franjo Tudjman."

"Well, I don't know – that's, that's – I mean, but, I really don't know if – if I'm up to a job like that. I mean, I just wrote this silly book about aliens."

True. It's called *The Official Alien Abductee's Handbook: How to Recover From Alien Abductions without Hypnotherapy, Crystals, or CIA Surveillance.*

In case you doubt, it is a humor book.

Jakov speaks like a man on a mission. "Oh, yes, you do great job. You tell American people his life. And you do great job for us."

I wonder what is really behind his mission. So I do what I usually do when I haven't a clue. "Well … can I get back to you?"

Over the weekend, I quickly research Tudjman. I read how he was jailed twice in the 1970s for speaking against the Yugoslav communists as part of the political rights movement called Croatian Spring. How in 1990, against huge odds, he forged the new nation of Croatia, independent from Yugoslavia.

Then I research the war that resulted from Croatia's separation. From the view of the international community, particularly the United States, Yugoslavia had to be preserved – but not at any great cost, and certainly not at the cost of military intervention. The US was still mopping up after the First Gulf War, and Eastern Europe was a bigger priority. As nations broke away from collapsing Soviet influence, the US feared this instability would spread throughout Europe.

I read how Tudjman led his newly independent country in battle against the Serbs, how he expelled the Serb citizens of Croatia, how he presided over the fight against the Serbs and Muslims in Bosnia. How he eventually garnered America's backing during the war, including the deployment of thousands of US and international troops now patrolling the area.

I read how he may or may not have planned to divide Bosnia in two. Then I read about the war atrocities committed by Croatian paramilitary. This guy Tudjman may not be Hitler – or Milosevic, for that matter – but he's no altar boy.

With each atrocity a blister appears in my mouth, followed by another, and another, until they fight each other for space. After a while I name them for areas with the most war crimes: Gospic, Ahmici, Stupni Do, Krajina …

I know then that I'll turn down the assignment. My body is rejecting it, even though my landlord would lobby for it. Maybe I could find a girlfriend who'd let me shack up with her when I get kicked out of my apartment.

On Monday I meet with Jakov.

"Jakov, I can't write this book."

"No, but Joe, you must. Only you must write book."

"Jakov, I can't write an official, glowing book about Tudjman. And even if I could, I wouldn't. I'd have no credibility. Why don't you hire a PR agency? There are lots of them in New York."

"No, Joe, you just write what you have to."

"But I can only do that if I have creative control over what's written."

"Yeah, of course, Joe. We give you."

"Are you sure? Do you know what you're saying?"

"You are a great artist. You make your view of his life. You can make a really great job."

I feel anxiety rising in me, the room shrinking, my stomach falling, but I can't think of a way out. "I want you to know that I'll be critical."

"Yeah, yeah. I know, but you can make great job. And we pay you $40,000."

"When do I go?"

What could be that hard about it? Gather some books, hire some researchers, do some interviews, a little cut-and-paste. Jakov even gives me a book to work from. Its title is in Croatian, but I imagine the translation: *Croatia: Democracy Fit for a King.*

I also imagine this as a career change towards international respectability. I would be a true historian, a word painter, swathing pages with sweeping descriptions of events and people, imbued with the weight of lasting importance. Alien books are fun, but this is significant, worthy of respect, self-worth, and hard cover. With this assignment I am groping towards legitimacy and merit.

But I am worried – really worried. Worried I'll make some huge historic or geographic blunder; that I'll become known as a paid propagandist for a repressive regime; that I'll get myself shot for shooting off my big mouth.

But I'm also excited: going on a journalistic assignment, even at the sponsorship of a nationalist government, I thrill to the challenge of discovering the truth about ancient rivalries and ethnic cleansing. I was to be given all the resources of the Croatian government, and free rein to write the official biography of its sitting president, Franjo Tudjman, the man who came out the big winner in the recent war in former-Yugoslavia, the man both vilified as a neo-fascist, and praised as a freedom fighter. No leader in central Europe has aroused this much controversy and passion.

I was about to unravel the Balkan onion, the mystery of the war between the Serbs, the Croats, and the Muslims, and the greater mystery of why the hell I was hired in the first place.

Chapter Two

"Good Morning, Paranoia"

> "If politics is power and power is everywhere,
> politics is in fact nowhere."
> – Hannah Arendt

"Oh, Joe, very soon I will see you in Croatia. I send you all information, airplane ticket. You will stay in Palace Hotel. Beautiful hotel. Which floor you like to stay?"

"I don't know."

"Please, Joe, any floor. Pick any floor."

"Well, okay. The sixth."

Jakov looks wounded. His face has fallen and taken on the dour look of a hurt lover.

"Joe," he says quietly. "Palace has only four floors."

"Then, any one. It doesn't matter to me. Any floor."

Immediately, Jakov brightens. "Okay, Joe. I see you there!" he shouts, pumping my hand as he leads me out the door.

It's only when I step outside the Croatian Embassy on Lexington Avenue in New York City that I realize I still haven't been paid my promised advance. Well, I console myself; at least he signed the agreement. For $300, my lawyer had drafted an i r o n c l a d agreement, giving me total editorial control, including the copyright should the book not be published within a year after submission.

"This is standard agreement?" Jakov had asked.

"Oh, yes, absolutely," I replied, sticking the pen in his hand. If he didn't come up with the money, I would be out $300, but no way would I front the airplane ticket, which hadn't arrived either.

The next day a check arrives at my door for $10,000. It is drawn on the Croatian bank account of the Zagreb National Theater.

When the check clears I head to a bookstore to make my first purchase of the month: $347.53 of books about the Balkans. "The fascist Tudjman," reads one. "Idi Amin of the Balkans," proclaims another. "Il Dulce of the Balkans," rants a third. Others are less kind. Tudjman inspires hatred. But also admiration – at least in the pamphlets Jakov doles out: "savior of his people," "freedom fighter," "founder of a new nation," "historian and statesman," and "his experience as a participant in the anti-fascist movement during the Second World War was crucial in forging peace in Bosnia and Herzegovina."

One glossy brochure speaks of the "indispensable partnership" between America and Croatia. America aided Tudjman in the war, pushed him to forge an alliance with the Bosnian Muslims in the fight against the Serbs, looked the other way while Croatia imported arms from Iran, deployed some 30,000 troops to NATO's peace-keeping operation in the region, and contributed millions of dollars in financial support to the struggling new nation. The US's stated objective was to achieve stability in southeast Europe, after the bloodiest war in the area since WWII, one that caused over 200,000 deaths and over one million refugees, with tens of thousands tortured and raped.

Yet criticism from the US government also hounds Tudjman: many see him as bearing an amount of responsibility for igniting the war, intransigent in efforts to re-integrate refugees, and downright belligerent on anything to do with the Bosnian Muslims. Were America's interests in preventing a failed Bosnian state – a state where Muslim terrorists could thrive – at odds with Tudjman's designs on Bosnia? Or were they stolidly aligned?

Less than halfway through the books I realize I need an objective road map, something to help me traverse the treacherous terrain of Balkan history and politics.

The following week, while I ponder the gaping hole of my international ignorance, a second $10,000 check arrives. This one is drawn from the American bank account of an Italian restaurant in Queens.

In addition to directing government-financed films, Jakov is a master in raising money from the Croatian diaspora, the ferociously loyal group of Croatian patriots whose $5,000 and $10,000 donations also helped import arms into their homeland during the war.

One young patriotic son of Croatian emigrants is George Rudman, a deceptively earnest Croatian-American, who responds to a notice I post at Columbia University for a paid researcher. In person, his unassuming and diligent manner contrasts with his vociferous opinions, which he laces with horror stories about his time in the war. George traveled to his parents' homeland to attend the country's first multiparty elections. Later, during the war, he worked as a translator for the Bosnian Croats during four years of international peace negotiations, often interpreting for Tudjman. He was also a driver for visiting diplomats, many so oblivious to the dangers of Central Bosnia that George had to physically restrain them from walking into minefields.

As one of those astute, articulate, and patriotic young American Croats from émigré families, George often feels that the Croats back in their homeland just don't get it. They don't get that you don't let rightwing, *Sieg Heil*-saluting extremists align themselves with your party and expect the US to understand. You don't rebury the bones of Ustasha leaders alongside their victims and expect world leaders to attend the ceremony (except for Germany). You don't honor indicted war criminals by decorating them as war heroes and expect recognition in the UN.

George was idealistic when he went to Croatia for the first time; he returned disillusioned and frustrated. American-style liberal democracy, he had learned, is not easily grafted onto the Balkan scene. He saw the high-level players who, with the best of intentions, could not implement policy on the ground: in particular when it came to human rights.

His war experience, however, never dampened his loyalty to his Croatian homeland, and its fight for independence – war crimes notwithstanding.

At first I'm thrilled to find someone so knowledgeable and accommodating to assist my venture by compiling a prep book, including timelines and a bibliographic "who's who in the Balkans"; and generally walking me through my own minefield of ignorance. But soon I wonder whether I can trust George as a source of information. Sitting at my kitchen table, I see the boyish face beneath prematurely thinning hair, watch his narrow eyes dart back and forth, as if fighting the urge to look over his shoulder for some unseen sniper or incoming mortar shell.

"The Croats never had a chance," George relates, *sotto voce*, "When the Serbs took over the Yugoslav army, Croatia was left with nothing but a couple of police vans and some World War Two rifles. Tudjman was the one with a vision, and the only one who was able to lead the country through the war and into independence."

"But don't you agree that ethnic cleansing—" I look closely for a response to the term, but, other than a blink, George betrays nothing. "—that ethnic cleansing was used in the war as a way to move populations and claim territory?"

"By the Serbs, oh yes."

"And by the Croats?"

"To a lesser extent."

Was it lack of motive, or lack of opportunity?"

"Opportunity, definitely." George seems to enjoy this part of the discussion. "Look at the history, Joe. All these wars were wars of reprisals. You kill my relative; I burn your house. You burn my house; I slaughter your village. But, Joe, these irreconcilable ancient rivalries are no different than those in Cyprus and Greece, Northern Ireland, or the Middle East. It's just the Balkans. The Balkans. And the Great Powers don't care about the Balkans. Until they can't control them."

George delivers his realpolitik with such knowing ease and chauvinistic humor that my suspicions melt away.

"By the way," I ask, pouring him another cup of coffee, "do you know a guy named Jakov Sedlar?"

"The film director? Yeah. Is he the one behind this deal?"

"He's arranging all my interviews."

He practically spits his java. "Oh, Christ, don't let him do that! You'll be given a tour of the presidential palace, a few drinks, and then they'll send you back to your hotel room."

"What else can I do? I don't know anyone there."

"I'll give you a list of names," George says, putting down his coffee and brandishing a pen. "Now, there's my buddy Ratko in the military …" Within minutes George has a page full of contacts in Croatia, some placed highly in the government, but none placed anywhere on Jakov's itinerary for me.

The following day, Jakov calls. For the first time I feel ahead of the game. I decide to keep my ace-in-the-hole, George, a secret from Jakov.

"Joe!" shouts Jakov. "I'm in Croatia. Can you hear?"

"Yes, you don't have to shout."

"Good," shouts Jakov. "You are making progress?"

"The research is going well."

"Good. It's good to have help."

"What?"

"I see you next week in Croatia. We have drink together."

"Yes, okay. Where—"

"I send you new itinerary tomorrow, or next day."

"Okay, but—"

"I must go. I call you later." Jakov sounds rushed. "Oh, and Joe?"

"Yes?"

"Please don't tell anyone about you writing book. Later I will explain. But please to promise. Okay?"

"Uh … yeah …"

"Okay. Goodbye, Joe!"

That night, taking a break from the stack of Balkan books, I scour the Internet and find a reprint of a newspaper article with the heading: *TUDJMAN HAS DEFINITELY SHOWN THAT HE IS A BRUTAL DICTATOR* – caps *sic*.

I manage to meet the author of the article, Roman Latkovic, now a political refugee in New York. Roman was a journalist from Croatia's only independent daily newspaper, *Novi List*, when he wrote his infamous article, in which he scurrilously blasted Tudjman for, among other things, labeling the Croatian opposition as Serb sympathizers. During a primetime broadcast on Croatian TV, several pro-government journalists attacked Latkovic as an "enemy of the state" who wanted to "liquidate the president." These comments were aired as the screen filled with Latkovic's photograph.

"But that was a very serious thing," says Latkovic, "because, you know, you have two hundred thousand people with arms in Croatia, and they are completely insane after the war, and they need enemies; they have no Chetniks or Serbs as a enemy, but now they have one single person who is an enemy; and after that madness start – because I received more than one thousand five hundred phone threats – it was recorded. And after that was a manhunt, and I was forced to hide."

After the death threats, a bomb went off in a car similar to his wife's car directly outside her home. The next day Roman received a phone call: "Next time we will not miss you and your Serbian whore." That's when he left for New York.

Deep paranoia still enveloped Croatia in 1996, one year after the war, when Roman's opinion piece was printed. While extremists were threatening his life, whipped up by the media who quoted Croatian officials suggesting that Serbia or Italian fascists were financing him, Tudjman loyalists, according to Latkovic, were phoning furiously to pressure him "not to use such harsh language," while other journalists complained that Latkovic was "stirring up trouble" for the rest of them.

"The slaves think that they have to do much more than boss require them to do," bemoans Latkovic, "and this is the worst part of Croatia."

Roman's words are representative of so much of the writing on

Croatia, and it unsettles me with the cumulative weight of world censure. I wonder how to reconcile the two images of Tudjman: the visionary freedom fighter versus the neo-Nazi war-mongerer. I now feel totally unprepared for this assignment. Do I really think I can take Jakov's money and turn in a fawning hagiography without becoming a whore? Or can I be ruthlessly critical in the manuscript without being a fraud?

Should I even take this assignment; am I stupidly putting myself at risk? If word gets out that I'm at work on a negative portrait of the president, will I be labeled an enemy spy, targeted for assassination, tortured or, worse – forced to refund Jakov's advance?

I had been introduced to Roman Latkovic by another Croatian living in America under political asylum: the unabashed communist, peace activist, body-builder, and genetically encoded troublemaker Ivo Skoric.

I first meet Ivo in a local New York restaurant, where he scarfs up a huge plate of pasta. I realize then that he is my anti-George. Born to a Serb mother and a Croat father, Ivo warns me – with a little too much enjoyment – about the widespread political surveillance and repression in his homeland.

Ivo is impish and loudmouthed; a prankster with a shaved head, ripped muscles, and certified asylum papers granting him US residency. His vocal criticisms of the Croatian government won him few friends there. Ivo offers assistance in arranging contact with journalists and peace activists.

"So, you're going to interview Tudjman?" Ivo shouts gleefully, pasta sauce dripping from his lips. "It will be a complete waste of your time. His aides will take you on a tour of Tito's villa, where he lives like a mini-dictator, give you a plate of fish, and then Tudjman will talk about great Croatia history and great Croatia destiny, but he won't admit he was ever really a communist even though he kissed Tito's ass for twenty years so much his lips are brown and sticky."

He scoops up another mouthful, and continues: "All the rank opportunists became nationalists overnight. So those who were supposedly well off in the previous regime now have to beg for mercy. It is actually more important that they are made to suffer for their past sins than that we get to actually enjoy ourselves." He laughs. He's really savoring this. "In Zagorje, the place where both Tito and Tudjman were born, there is ancient expression: 'May God strike dead my neighbor's cow.' That is Croatia."

I recall Jakov's familiar refrain whenever I bring up controversial Croatian issues: "Joe, small country – big problem."

So, now I have George on the right and Ivo on the left. Logically I should trust Ivo less than I trust George. George works for a prestigious New York investment bank, while Ivo teaches snowboarding in Vermont. George's contacts are prominent government and business leaders; Ivo's are disaffected dissidents. But while I try to make as many contacts as I can with George's connections, Ivo's are more fun. I mustn't let Ivo know I'm cozying up too much with the government in Zagreb. After all, I still don't know the good guys from the bad.

"Joe," advises Ivo, "you should be practicing your Croatian. Now, repeat after me: '*Idemo vodite Ljubav.*'"

I work on the phrase until he's satisfied with my pronunciation.

"Okay," I ask impatiently, "now tell me what it means."

"It's just the most useful phrase you'll ever need in Croatia: 'Let's make love.'"

Ivo has me pegged; he knows my motivation. I'm that transparent. To him I'm just another American voyeur, a war tourist, on a cheap flight for cheap thrills. I warn myself not to let my authorial ambitions become a cover for casual sex and fleeting fame. A warning easier said than done.

I should approach this project with the seriousness and gravitas it deserves. I should take my cue directly from the people who have lived through the horrors of the war. People like George, who, a few days later, rings me in a late-night call.

"Hey Joe, you old wop guinea. When are you gonna have a drink with me?" It's the first time I've heard George soused.

"Hi, George. You sound pretty happy."

"What are you doing; reading more books?" he slurs. "You gotta get out."

"I was out last night."

"With your intellectual, artsy friends? You gotta milk this trip to Cro, man. Make some money."

"I want to make money. I used to make money with my business, till I got divorced."

"Oh, so you're a Jew!"

"Look, George, I'll see you tomorrow, okay? Meanwhile, have some coffee and go to mass."

I know George is playing the Balkan version of ethnic baiting, but I'm not game. The only Balkan jokes more prevalent than those involving Jews, Orthodox Serbs, and Catholic Croats, are those involving Muslims. And George knows them all.

I do give him a lot of slack. In the heart of Bosnia at its darkest hour, George had more than once barely escaped death at the hands of the Bosnian Serbs. He was my history professor, sounding board, and contact manager.

But the more I listen to George, the more I hear the voice of Mate Boban, the deceased leader of the Bosnian Croats, for whom George had ostensibly worked as a press agent during the war.

Had Boban lived, the International War Crimes Tribunal at The Hague surely would have named him as the most-wanted Croat war criminal. As president of the Bosnian Croats, Boban never had the opportunity of killing as many civilians as his Bosnian Serb brothers in Christ. That personal best was achieved by Radovan Karadzic, co-founder of the Serbian Democratic Party, who was charged with genocide for killing up to 8,000 Muslims in Srebrenica. Until his arrest in 2008, Karadzic was the most wanted Balkan war criminal. By March of 2016, he would be found guilty of genocide, war crimes and crimes against humanity, and be sentenced to 40 years' imprisonment.

Like Karadzic, however, Boban did rule a para-state, where concentration camps and ethnic cleansing flourished. Among his inner circle, I am told Boban's nickname was "the Mobster."

Also known as "John Gotti from Herzegovina," the Mobster was fiercely loyal to Franjo Tudjman. Everyone who knew Boban said the same thing: he worshipped Tudjman like a god, and saw him as the savior of the Croatian people.

I hear rumors that Boban is still alive, hiding somewhere in the Balkans, but George dismisses it as total nonsense – and then defends Boban, but in a Balkan way, as one might defend a dear relative with a penchant for revenge killings.

"George," I ask, having practiced this question for days, "in Bosnia, it seems, both the Serbs and the Croats fought the Muslims for control of Bosnia. The Serbs had their death camps, and so did the Croats. And you worked for the president of the Bosnian Croats, Mate Boban, right?"

"Joe, Boban always put national interests first." He seems more than ready for my question. "I worked as a translator during four years of international peace negotiations, right beside Boban. I was idealistic and naïve, but I was stoked. Then I saw all the contingents of international so-called peace negotiators pile in by the planeload. They had no idea of what was going on down on the ground. These guys were appeasing the Serbs, the first aggressors in this war; all the while we're being shot at by Serb snipers as I'm driving them like a madman through Sarajevo."

He continues, now as fired-up as he must have been in the war: "These guys did not and could not implement policy on the ground. And they all talk so grandly about human rights. Just where do you gather an effective, efficient fighting force from a civilian population overnight? Where else but the black marketers, thugs, and killers-for-hire? How come there weren't *more* atrocities should really be the question."

"Okay George, I didn't mean to get you riled up, but there are all these books I keep reading that paint Tudjman as a dictator."

"They're all anti-Croat propaganda." He is practically spitting now. "Those Brit authors still think they are back in World War II, noble heroes of the Berlin Airdrop. They don't realize that this time the Serbs were the aggressors."

"So I shouldn't be reading all these books I bought – just your briefing book?"

"Yeah, sure. But all you need to remember, Joe, is that every leader there – Tudjman, Milosevic, Izetbegovic – is a former communist, now turned nationalist."

George does have one final word of warning. "Joe, watch out for the women. All the women in Zagreb are, like, five-ten. If you want to score, you're gonna have to try some old-fashioned Italian imperialism, gumba."

"What's the legal age of consent in Zagreb?

"Same as in any other country: whatever you get away with." He's starting to fade now. "I have to warn you, my fine American friend, to just watch out for the women. They're dangerous."

Immediately after I hang up on our drunk-dialing session, I conduct a mental inventory: Croatia, a country that fought an unrelenting war for four years, lost hundreds of thousands of lives, had war heroes and war criminals, bombs, bullets, death, and destruction – and the *women* he says are dangerous? I gotta go there!

Chapter Three

"Back to School"

> "Real knowledge is to know the extent of one's ignorance."
> **– Confucius**

"What is your name again? I never heard of you. Are you with the university?" Yale professor Ivo Banac is widely known as a leading Croatian historian, and part-time politician. After I hire George, I reach out to the notoriously prickly professor by phone for another point of view.

"No, Professor, I'm a commercial author looking to hire a researcher for my book about Tudjman. Would you be interested in the assignment?"

"Are you a historian?"

"I've done some research—"

"Do you speak Croatian?"

"Well, I've picked up a few phrases—"

"Have you ever been to Croatia?"

"Ah—No, but— I'm going there next week."

"What kind of book is this going to be? Because you sound like a dilettante with no idea of the history of the Balkans, let alone the regional, ethnic, and cultural variances. Who is publishing this so-called book?"

"HarperCollins."

"Who is your editor?"

"I'm working with Jakov Sedlar – at the Croatian consulate."

His voice crackles through the phone. "Sedlar? That rank propagandist?"

"Oh, you know Jakov?" I try to counter his obduracy with headstrong cheeriness.

"I don't know who you are, but you are miserably unqualified to write any book on the Balkans. And if Mr. Sedlar is in any way involved with this amateur undertaking, this book will most certainly be a total embarrassment and you will become an international laughingstock." He hangs up with no cheeriness at all.

There, that was the encouragement I was looking for.

Chapter Four

"Diplomatic Ignominy"

> "Tell the truth and run."
> **– Old Yugoslav proverb**

At the airport, everyone looks like they lead a double life. I gaze down the line of faces, speculating: a businessman trying to purchase interests in the Balkans before they get privatized and bought for cheap by Croatian government insiders, a Croatian student returning home from a semester of English classes and house painting, a drug smuggler, a foreign aid worker, and a man who I'm sure must work for the CIA, though he says he is a journalist. Dressed in an open Hawaiian shirt and khaki shorts, this ruddy-faced pot-bellied man, already drunk, displays small knowledge and smaller interest in Balkan politics. But there is something about him that keeps me wondering. Is he reticent to share information because he's drunk, or because the information he holds is some valuable, tightly guarded secret?

As soon as the plane takes off, the man falls asleep, and I resume reading George's briefing book, which contains colorful descriptions of the people I would soon interview: "Mate Granic, Foreign Minister, nickname: 'The Little Monk.' A medical doctor and pacifist who will probably go back to private practice after Tudjman dies, since he has no support among the hard-liners …" I alternate between reading the briefing book and books on ancient and modern Balkan history.

There are disturbing parallels here, not so much in "ancient hatreds," that smutty old chestnut used by the victors in their history rewrites, but in the iron grip that myth and the manipulation of myth has over the region.

I am going to break that tradition, I promise myself, like a glass doll thrown headfirst into a stone quarry. I am going to bring back the dirt, the real story behind the war, the hatred, the violence; I am going to reveal the dirty secret alliances, the dark conspiracies, and the foul complicities; I will reveal it all – as soon as I figure out who are the Serbs and who are the Croats.

In Vienna I change planes boarding a small propeller aircraft. A tall, lissome woman sits next to me, her legs stretching all the way into first class. Jadranka was named for the Adriatic, but her attitude is anything but serene. She is 26, with short dark hair and a crooked smile that could turn from sweet to sour in a second. On the flight to Zagreb I keep thinking, "Boy, they grow 'em tall here."

"I don't care much for politics," she says in near-perfect English. "I know that there is a much greater difference now between rich and poor. There is no more middle class in Croatia."

Jadranka is one of many urban Croats who have seen the economic power in their country shift all the way up to the top. She thinks more reform is happening, but only for private companies. And many of them have ties to Tudjman.

But she is also critical of her country's workforce: "In America, the people are always striving for things. Here, they do not like work. Here they are stuck in the communist thinking."

She notes the regional rivalries within her own country. "The people in Istria think the people in Zagreb are shit, because they live in the city and not along the coast. We in Zagreb think they are too envious of the Italians. Sometimes I wish I lived there. I don't want to live in Croatia."

Then, remembering I hold an American passport, she leans over and smiles. "Hey, Joe, whatcha gonna do?"

"That's good American slang, Jadranka."

"I learned it from my ex-American boyfriend. He is shit."

"Well, I'm sorry."

"It is true. So ... whatcha gonna do?"

"How about dinner later?"

She smiles, accepting my invite. This bodes well. Before I even land, I'm scoring dates.

Entering Zagreb, I see a country struggling for a sense of identity. In the taxi, Croatian Radio blares the news with over-modulated urgency, while outside, the sad edifices of 1970s public housing fly by – lone outposts girding the older, once-imperious, central city.

"Zagreb," I write in my notebook, "has all the feel of a lumbering, bungling, slightly deranged distant cousin who no one admits being related to. Even the sky feels suspended, somehow missing the chill of the communist northern gusts, waiting for the warm wind of capitalism to ease its fevered pain."

I check into the Palace Hotel: old, borderline seedy, once-imperial – where the managers pipe Lounge Musak into the elevators, unaware that, in America's urban hot-spots, its revival has become hip. This out-of-it-ness is part of Zagreb's dozy charm. Or maybe I'm just jet-lagged.

I change clothes without showering and head to the American Embassy. There, in the light airy office filled with dark and heavy wood furniture I meet Douglas Davidson, official title: Information Officer, American Embassy to Croatia. I let him know I'm here and what I'm doing. He seems intrigued, if a bit perplexed. Fresh from the Ivy vine, soft-spoken and smooth, Doug doesn't know why the Croatians hired me, but he does find it extremely amusing that I am not a historian. It's a good thing I didn't tell him about my alien book.

He confirms Tudjman's tight control of the media, and how this is hampering the return of the Croatian Serbs into the country. "When we speak with the Croatian government," Doug says, "we constantly tell them: 'We're not saying you have to let 90% of the Serbs back.' We're saying, 'if you want to join the Western community you can't deny people the right to return to their homes. It's a fundamental human right.'" He crosses his legs, and asks "You didn't mention a publisher for your book. Will this be a university press or a trade publication?"

"It's for the popular market, so HarperCollins will be publishing it." At least that was what Jakov had told me. Douglas doesn't react, but his silence speaks loudly. I feel my throat tighten. "Actually," I continue needlessly, "I was asked by a Croatian film director to write the book."

"Really?"

"Jakov Sedlar."

"He's the cultural attaché."

"Yes, and he's given me total editorial control."

"How … very … curious …" Doug weighs the words as he speaks. "Did he tell you how the book is going to be used?"

"Well, I believe in making current and historical events understandable. Foreign affairs is my first love—"

He politely coughs, as if on cue. "There's a large diaspora that consumes anything Croatian. I'm also thinking about what we here call 'The Image Problem.'"

"Oh," I jump in like a contestant on *Jeopardy!* "You mean neo-Nazism, domestic suppression, and war crimes. I'm leaving in all the juicy parts," I say proudly.

Douglas seems incredulous, shakes his head. "Well, let's arrange to have you meet the Ambassador on, say, Thursday, at noon." He makes a note in his schedule book.

"Thanks. That would be great." I stand, sensing it's my time to depart. But Doug remains seated, calmly continuing the discussion, leaving me to awkwardly shift from foot to foot.

"This is a most interesting project, Joe. So little correct information about Tudjman makes it to the Croatian people; so little information about Croatia makes it to the States. I assume you'll want to interview some native journalists while you're here."

"Of course." For some reason, images of bearded men in torn jeans being tortured with sharpened knives flash through my mind.

Doug then guides me to a small TV. "So, we will see you again on Thursday. Here's a short tape with some of the Ambassador's highlights. It was a pleasure." He shakes my hand, and departs.

Ambassador Peter Galbraith has lean sunken eyes and an angular jaw that juts to whomever he is addressing. His perpetually scruffy hair and rumpled suit make him appear more like a disheveled high-school mathematics teacher than America's official representative to a foreign nation. Yet he is forceful in his speech on Croatian TV: "I am a great friend of the Croatian people, their culture, and their heritage," he says to a small crowd of local journalists, "but President Tudjman caused serious harm to the Serb minorities in his country, and America will not stand by even their closest friend and simply watch as atrocities take place ..."

For much of the war, the American people knew little and cared less about the Balkans. The ones who were aware were split among those who wanted no US political or military involvement in an area rife with religious and ethnic strife, those who saw the conflict as a spark that could ignite a larger conflagration consuming Europe itself, and those who believed we had a moral and humanitarian imperative to stop genocide in our time.

Only when mortar victims in Sarajevo were broadcast on CNN did larger America become more aware. The dead were innocent shoppers at a market square, dressed like any American shopper, and torn to pieces.

Those images replay in my head on my walk back to the hotel; my thoughts turning on words like guilt, responsibility, truth, and integrity. Placed in this position, having accepted this assignment, here in the middle of Zagreb, divorced from the familiarity of New York, with no obligations and no responsibilities, except the largest one I have ever shouldered, I am more than ready. For in my mind, I have secretly transferred the assignment from the hands of the Tudjman regime into those of the Croatian, Bosnian, and Serbian people. Once I seal this pact, I find the confidence and, surprisingly, the courage, to take on what feels increasingly like a grateful obligation.

✳ ✳ ✳

Word travels fast in the Balkans. Back at the Palace Hotel, I call a potential interviewee.

"*Dobra dan*, hello. This is Joe Tripician, I want to speak with Vlado—"

"Oh, yes, Mr. Joe Tripician. We heard you were here. We were wondering when you'd call."

"But I didn't tell you I was here."

"Yes. We know. Welcome to Croatia!"

Chapter Five

"Bloody History"

> "Only three things grow here: snakes, stones and Ustashas."
> **– Western Herzegovian expression**

"Mommy, where is daddy?"

"In jail, dear."

The three-year-old looks quietly at his mother. Most things puzzle him. Some things can't be spoken about outside their home.

Daddy is in jail again for political reasons. Everything in the Tudjman household revolves around politics. Stjepan Tudjman is often imprisoned for his political activities with the Croatian Peasant Party, which consists of organizing the dirt-poor farmers in the village in a resistance struggle. Sometimes, when Stjepan returns, his wife Justina tends the wounds he received from being beaten in prison. Four years later, she dies. Franjo would then care for his two brothers at home. And wait.

So begins the first draft of my book, the "official biography" of Franjo Tudjman. But I need an insight, some privileged scoop to get inside the man's skin. Is the clue to this his father? And his father's idols?

The Croatian Peasant Party (the HSS), his father's party, was led by the charismatic Stjepan Radic. A cross between Gandhi and Huey Long, Radic fought to give the Croat peasants representation in the Serb-dominated parliament – plus the right to own the land they till. This radical position provided him with no shortage of enemies, and he was soon assassinated.

"This goes too much into historic shit for me." Even through his email I can feel Ivo's spittle. I keep up a daily electronic correspondence with him from my dusty room in Zagreb's Palace Hotel.

"Just so I understand, Ivo: one of daddy Tudjman's closest friends joins the Ustasha, the gang of Croat nationalists soon backed by the Nazis. This family friend later attempts but fails to assassinate King Alexander. Young Tudjman joins the communist-led Partisans, and after the war he moves into the Yugoslav Army, but later is jailed for his nationalist writings."

"Oh, Joe, I saw you on Croatian TV," Ivo emails me. "A fine performance. You are now really great friend of Croatian George Washington, eh?"

"That— that was edited out of context."

"I thought so. But too late for you, Joe. Everyone knows you now as huge supporter of Tudjman and his suppression of media and dissent."

"Let's stay on topic, Ivo. Back when Franjo's mother dies, his father becomes even more active in politics, eventually recruiting his son to hand out banned pamphlets via bicycle on a thirty-kilometer trek.

'How dare you give a child pamphlets?' a political comrade berates his father, as the young Franjo watches wide-eyed – or so I imagine. 'If they catch him, he'll give us all up!'

'Yes,' his father replies, 'he may be a child, but he is my son.'

"My question, Ivo, is: how much of a communist really was Tudjman?"

"Joe, he was the youngest Yugoslav Army general and I never completely comprehended the reasons of his speedy rise. Perhaps he was a snitch, maybe he told communists about HSS officials who cooperated with Ustasha, maybe he told about his Serb Partisan colleagues who plotted against Tito with Chetniks – he had to do something unbelievably dirty to get to be a general at 23 – don't you think so?" Conjecture flows from Ivo like plum brandy at a Croatian feast. Evidence, however, is as scant as salad on the same table.

Ivo's on a rolling rant now. "He is vain, arrogant, and controlling. By the way he runs the country and his family, he is an autocratic clan leader. In my observation, he is very much like my father." Ivo's emails, like Ivo himself, are always entertaining.

This chain is getting long. "Ivo, as you continue to remind me, Tito and Tudjman both come from the same town – birthplace of very few Partisans. So who were the other local communists from Tudjman's hometown?"

"How could I possibly know that on the top of my head? All this research, consulting, and information development supplied by the Ivo, Inc. by now far exceeds the plate of pasta, so I will have to make the Joetrip, Inc. do a lot of video work for Ivo, Inc. (I have some ideas, already, hehehe)."

"I'm happy to help, Ivo."

"While you are in Zagreb you can call up my family, Joe. You could get my brother Nikola to show you his sanctuary if you pretend that you are an American rightwing militia type seeking those just-right connections in the emerging democracies of Eastern Europe."

"I'll keep his number handy."

Many unsubstantiated rumors swirl around Tudjman's activities during the period when the Partisans were liberating Zagreb in May of '45. Accusers say Tudjman and his father were involved in the murder of the "local spies" Stjepan Tudjman railed against. Despite the lack of evidence, the last US Ambassador to Yugoslavia, Warren Zimmermann, confided to me that Tudjman "was probably associated with political murders for the communist regime."

I take a late-night walk on the deserted, narrow streets of Zagreb. My mind is bouncing between history and women. Must every country's political landscape be plagued by the repeated mistakes of war? What dysfunctional pattern am I repeating that is setting me up for yet another fall? How sad and funny that it takes more courage to face your own fears than to plop yourself down in a war-torn zone and pretend you're searching for the truth while hiding from it.

"Did you hook up with any babes yet, Joe?"

We communicate via email, but I can hear George's smirk across the pond.

"No comment, George, just help me out here. Is this correct: 'After the assassination of Radic, the HSS party's leader, he is succeeded by the less volatile, but just as determined, Vladko Macek, a friend of the Tudjman family.

"'When Tudjman is just fifteen, his father takes him on a visit to Macek. Young Franjo watches as the two men passionately discuss politics and Croatian history dating back into the medieval era of Croat kings.

"'Two years later, Macek strikes a deal that gives autonomy to Croatia, and power sharing to the Serbs, at the expense, as happens so often in Balkan politics, of the other Yugoslavs. Much of Bosnia-Herzegovina is given to Croatia.

"'The Macek agreement is the first between the Serbs and the Croats that divides the territory of Bosnia-Herzegovina between them, and this forms the basis for young Franjo's moral and political belief system. He would hold to this vision when negotiating with Milosevic to divide Bosnia between them.'"

"Yeah, Joe, you got it right."

By this time I'm not really surprised at George's response. While modern nationalists publicly refute Tudjman's goal of a divided and ethnically pure Bosnia as fantasy, George embraces it as reality.

"In the end, Joe, it seems that Tudjman was right for maintaining secret ties with Milosevic and not allowing Izetbegovic to gain full control of Bosnian Croat military forces."

Like they say, you can't argue with success.

Tudjman's father falls out of favor with the new regime. It happens, according to Tudjman, on a warm April day in '46, in his own quiet village, in his own quiet home. Tito's secret police enter the house and shoot his father and his stepmother. The official story is suicide – communist jargon for murder.

"Of course, I could never accept this particular version," says Tudjman. "I knew about my father's dissatisfaction with the regime, and therefore I had suspicions. For quite a few years after that I did hear some rumors, but it was only in the '80s that I definitely found out the names of the people who had murdered my father and stepmother … I'm not going to mention any names, because members of their family are still alive, but their names, if they could be made public, would be very interesting for the people involved."

Knowing that Franjo's son Miroslav now heads the Croatian intelligence service makes it even more interesting.

I wonder if this search for the truth compels Tudjman to seek justice, or what he considers justice in his post-communist, fledgling democracy. During Tito's reign, justice was meted out at Naked Island, an oversized rock quarry on the Adriatic that held about twelve thousand men and women who were regularly beaten and abused. As part of their "rehabilitation," prisoners on Naked Island were expected to confess and recant their sins against the Yugoslav Communist Party. For Tudjman to seek personal justice for his father's murder I conclude is a given; how he will accomplish this is uncertain.

For the people of Croatia, Serbia, and Bosnia – the victims of the war – for those who seek the truth, where is their justice? Will confessions, convictions, and jail time at The Hague Tribunal be enough, or does that fail miserably to compensate for their collective and individual suffering? And if so, will they go to war to get their justice? And how far will that war spread?

When asked what would set off the next wide war in Europe, German Chancellor Bismarck responded prophetically: "Some damn foolish thing in the Balkans."

Chapter Six

"Today We Have Lunch at the Mass Graves"

"God save me from Serb heroism and Croatian culture."
– **Miroslav Krleza, Croatian author**

During the day, Jakov arranges for me to interview government officials from almost every single department, one after another after another. Never have I been lied to by so many people in such a short period of time. And they all want to explain, very politely, about the true cause of ethnic rivalries that started only recently – if you call the eleventh century recent.

In the Balkans, everyone says: "We can't talk on the phone. Meet me in the Square at 12 o'clock." So here I stand in the center of Josip Jelacic Square, a French beret on my head, wondering if I look too much like a target.

At the square I interview the young kids. They look at me suspiciously in this post-war climate of profiteers, kidnappers, spies, and informers. I have lumbered into the Balkans, a blundering American character from a Graham Greene novel: determined to save this land while destined only to make things worse.

In Zagreb, the silent masses of walking citizens are ever obedient to the pedestrian crossing lights even when there is no traffic. They pass by the hip-hop/punk/Benetton-styled teenagers who rollerblade across the square, looking only as far ahead as the next tram, which arrives like clockwork, taking folks to and from a city that still has to remind the rest of the world that it is part of Europe. Disillusionment is strongest among the young, the under-30 crowd, called "the Doomed Generation."

Lana is a 17-year-old student, with black-painted fingernails as chipped as the green paint lacquered on her boots. Her father switched from being a journalist to a traveling salesman because the pay was better. Also, says Lana, "Being a journalist in Croatia is not very good. You have to write what they tell you to write. All the news in the papers and on TV is all lies. Everything they say is bullshit." Lana wants to study chemistry, but she doesn't know what profession she'll eventually choose. She does know it won't be medical, because the pay is so low.

One 16-year-old student, in baggy jeans, a deck of playing cards on her lap, had a bad experience in the hospital after a fall. The doctor rushed her treatment because, she feels, he wasn't getting paid enough and resented having to work for it. "Now there is not so much money for schools and hospitals," she says. "I cannot play sports again. The government is not doing enough for the people."

Mario, 24, works for his father in construction, although there's not enough to pay a living wage these days. "Oh, I think the government is great," he says, turning red and laughing at his own sarcasm. "I work longer now than I ever did for even less now than I ever had," and laughs again, this time not as loudly. "During the war I was in school. I've never been out of the country. I plan to stay. What choice do I have?" He seems weary now, at having to voice the details of his dead-end life. Excusing himself, he grabs his girlfriend, and they rush off down the alley.

* * *

The sun is setting as I stroll further up the square, on a cobblestone street lined with outdoor cafés. Several fashionable customers have already settled in the choicest seats, with quick access to the attentive waiters and the eyes of available passersby. I am counting the minutes to my dinner date, contemplating what led me to this place and time, all the while recounting what forces propelled Tudjman into historical prominence.

In 1989, Tudjman established the first democratic party in Croatia, and reintroduced Ustasha flags and symbols to the streets of Zagreb, calling them ancient symbols of the Croatian state, years after Croatia's image had been tarnished by the events of that Nazi-backed gang.

The war in the 1990s began when Croatia and Slovenia seceded from Yugoslavia, and the central government fought back, commandeering the Yugoslav army (the JNA) and inciting the Serb minority in Croatia to rebel. It had been years since Tudjman was a desk general in the JNA, and he would soon miscalculate the actions of his old army buddies, whom he thought wouldn't attack when Croatia declared independence. By 1991, the first shots were fired, and Croatia lost over a third of its territory to the JNA and rebel Serb forces. Tudjman was about to go down in history as the first democratically elected president of Croatia – and the last.

Under Serbian strongman Slobodan Milosevic ("the Butcher of the Balkans"), both Croatia and the more homogeneous Slovenia were labeled fascists, and, for a time after the war started, the label stuck. My assignment appears to be a big rehabilitation job.

In the eyes of the West, nationalism in the former Yugoslavia was a bad thing, responsible for the bloody war of ethnic cleansing. For Franjo Tudjman and his supporters, Croatian nationalism meant a road out of 35 years of stifling communism and a century of second-class citizenship. Nationalism is patriotism, and in that sense the war in the former Yugoslavia becomes a civil war, proving again that close relatives always fight the fiercest.

* * *

"Why are we going to your hotel room? I have to go home."

"We had a lovely dinner, a nice walk. I thought you'd like a drink from my wet bar. Jakov is paying for all of it." I give her my most charming smile, but Jadranka isn't easily conned. She's suspicious that I'll just blow into town and then blow out again, which is, of course, exactly what I intend to do.

She suddenly quizzes me about her country.

"What are Ustasha?"

"They were the Nazi-puppet regime in Croatia under Ante Pavelic."

She nods, not totally impressed. "And what are Chetniks?"

"They were the Serbian guerilla force under Draza Mihailovic, who eventually collaborated with the Italians and the German-controlled, Serb-run government in Serbia."

"Yes. And what caused war today?"

"Well, when Milosevic took control of the JNA and incited Serb militants, there was a massive imbalance in firepower when Serbia first attacked—"

"Okay," she admits, "you will write a good book."

Then we enter my hotel room.

"Oh, I see." She practically shouts as she enters the room. "Mr. Double-Bed! Why do you need a double bed, Mr. Double-Bed?"

"It's just what they gave me. I didn't ask for it. I use it to spread out my books, and—"

"I think you have some other plan in mind, Mr. Double-Bed."

"No, look. Let's just have a drink, and then you can go home."

"I think I go home now."

"Don't go. I'm lonely here."

"Is that the only reason you want me to stay, because you are lonely?"

Ouch. "No, of course not. I like you."

"Well … I can't make love to you. What if I fall in love?"

I don't have an answer for that. It isn't in my phrase book.

Later, I realize I should have responded: "Well, what if I fall in love with you?" But that would be giving too much away. A bad and often lethal habit in the Balkans.

Jadranka and I meet for a number of dinners on Jakov's dime. She tells me of her brother who used to work in construction and wants to be a banker, but who spends his days drinking and watching TV. I fight the urge to grab her in my arms, lose myself in a maddening embrace, flinging myself into an unknowable future. Anything to enflame her hope and erase my past.

At the end of my Croatian tour, we have our last dinner together in the center of Zagreb, over several bottles of Italian wine, and she swears she isn't at all enamored of me.

"You are kind American, Joe," she says, "but I don't really love you. I couldn't love you, not at all."

"Well – okay. How's your dinner?"

"You have to take sides, Joe."

"What do you mean?"

"You have to write with point of view, how this country is corruption, how America watched as war start and did nothing, how you come here to tell us what to do and you know nothing. We want your help, we don't want you here, now go."

"Oh – you want me to take sides, but you want me to go?"

"Yes, everyone must take sides. And no, you must not go—" She now softens, gives me that crooked smile, "until you get me job at American Embassy."

After getting no more than a kiss from her, I promise to do what I can. I'm such an easy mark. No matter. I can't get her a job at the embassy; I have to maintain my journalistic impartiality. They'll think I've gone native.

I worry a lot about what others think, and what they might do. Will I be attacked as a propagandist, or as a muckraker? Will I trust the wrong people, or will my next trust be betrayed? This is why I feel the need to go incognito, for fear that I will be revealed as a charlatan or instigator.

My mission, now that have I accepted, is known to everyone I interview. My secret, however, is known to a select few; many would not be willing to discuss Tudjman, especially if they knew the Croatian government was behind it, my "creative control" notwithstanding.

Jakov gives me free rein – almost too much free rein. From my room in the Palace Hotel I plan, meet, and interview whomever I want, trying to track down the dirt – any dirt. I discover a pattern of propaganda and political agendas designed to make Tudjman look bad. His image as a neo-Nazi never outstrips the facts of Serbian aggression.

Anyone with any connection to the former Yugoslavia has deeply felt convictions, and it is easier to identify the allegiance of those with whom I speak than to discover the real truth. This operative reveals a recurring pattern in the political behavior of former Yugoslav citizens. Attribute it to socialist-induced laziness, fear of deviation from the norm, or the hold history has on the region. Is this the reason Jakov hires me, a New York writer and documentary producer with no ethnic, political, or ideological connections to ex-Yugo? Perhaps. Or perhaps it is his government's belief that no dirt on their President will turn up.

I'll just have to keep digging.

* * *

The following day I'm in the hotel dining room, surrounded by cheese, beef, pork, sausages, and plum wine: the typical Balkan breakfast. Then Jakov enters.

"Joe, good morning! Oh, such a light breakfast, please to have more."

"No, I really couldn't, thanks."

"Joe, big day today. Today you meet President."

"Today?"

"Yes, but first we have lunch – at mass graves. Come!"

He drags me outside into a waiting black sedan, where we speed off at 90 miles per hour to a small airport and a smaller helicopter. It's an old Russian Mi8-MTV-1 chopper used for transport by the Croatian Air Force during the war. Jakov crawls up front to sit next to the pilot. I climb in the rear and sit next to two rabbis, invited guests of the Croatian government, which is trying to ease relations with the Jewish people.

"I met him, and I don't think he's anti-Semitic or neo-Nazi, or in any way sympathetic to Nazism. I didn't see any of that," says Rabbi Jack Bemporad, Director of the Center for Christian Jewish Understanding.

"What about his book, *The Horrors of War?*" I ask Jack, over the shuddering din inside the chopper.

"A good deal of the sources that he uses I would say are not the best or the most objective sources, but given what he had to work with, given where he was, and given the kind of education people got under communism and even before that, I would say that that would be probably normal. You can't expect him to be sensitive to the sort of things that it took Vatican II and 30 years of dialogue to bring about."

Drat, no dirt. How will I get anyone to read my book if there's no sensationalism? I am also worried about being labeled pro-Ustasha. In the Balkans, labels get attached easier than mud on a UN tank, and soon you find yourself an enemy of a people, a government, or both. One American researcher who worked on the book made me swear I'd never use his name, citing the flak he'd receive if it were published. "I don't like to be involved in political discussions with people who scream and yell at you," he explained.

Our helicopter flies over scenic Vukovar by the Danube: vacation spot of choice for Eastern Europeans, sympathetic socialists, and Germans.

In Croatia the war began with the return of ethnic cleansing: its goal was to move the non-Serb/non-Orthodox population out of their homes through acts of unimaginable terror. Villages were burnt to the ground or bombarded, and hundreds fled into neighboring villages and far-away towns carrying nothing but the clothes on their backs.

Denied access to the Adriatic through Gospic, the Serbs pushed westward from Slavonia. Then, in scenic Vukovar, the Serbs laid siege, bombing it continuously for 87 days.

At the end of the three-month bombardment, nothing remained but the shells of gaping buildings.

In one of the first acts of terror, Serb irregulars marched in, rounded up the survivors, released the women and children, and massacred some 300 men in a hospital. Their bodies were dumped into a shallow grave near the village of Ovcara. Today, with camera crew in tow, Jakov leads the rabbis and me to it.

We stand at the foot of the barren field, hidden from the main dirt road outside of Vukovar, the cameras jostling for position, going in close for a sound bite. The rabbis speak eloquently about inhumanity, compassion, and memory, while I stand back, trying to distance myself from a potential Jakov sideshow.

I feel a pressure. A giant wave is pushing me from this scene too large to comprehend. One tall Croat soldier, standing nearby with his semi-automatic pinned to his chest, taps me on the back. He speaks briefly in Croatian, gesturing to the surrounding fields. I think he is showing me where to go to get out of camera shot, and I start moving in that direction.

For some reason this only makes him speak louder and gesture more broadly, and I respond by moving quicker. That's when Jakov lunges over and grabs me, hauling me back to the van.

"No, Joe, this way," he says calmly, friendly. "You want to stay away from landmines."

That's just the way he said it: like I was caught jaywalking – jaywalking into 800 thousand landmines. I have to be careful not to blow myself up – at least before I write the story.

But first I have to find the story, while still being a guest of Jakov and his government, and remaining independent and keeping editorial control – and staying out of trouble.

And keeping the label "paid propagandist" from sticking to me. As for Tudjman, he labels all dissenting voices as unpatriotic. He is thin-skinned to criticism, and hence easy to lampoon, as the Croatian satirical magazine *The Feral Tribune* proves every week.

When *Feral* ran an issue showing a faked photomontage of Tudjman and Milosevic in bed naked together, Tudjman hit the roof. The editors faced a seditious libel suit for insulting the President, which, in Croatia's amendment to the criminal law, is illegal.

The article at issue was "Bones in the Mixer." It ridiculed Tudjman's proposal of "national reconciliation" to rebury the remains of the Ustasha leaders alongside the remains of their victims in Jasenovac: "Croatia's biggest underground city," says the headline. Then it compared Tudjman with the Spanish dictator Francisco Franco.

Lawsuits and late-night phone calls seem to be the preferred methods of pressuring the independent media in Croatia. In this, Franjo Tudjman never learns that cracking down on his critics gives them more visibility – to their defenders and their detractors.

Meanwhile, as we drive to the presidential house, I struggle to erase that image of naked political coitus from my mind.

Chapter Seven

"In Tito's Shadow"

> "Why should I be a minority in your country,
> when you can be a minority in mine?"
> **– Modern Balkan expression**

The ride to the Presidential Residence is scenic. The winding road is carved into a meticulously maintained forest and leads upwards to a hill with an understated stone sculpture. It resembles a nature conservatory, only with armed plain-clothed security, metal detectors, and overly costumed Palace Guards, decked out in red and gold, with bayoneted rifles and fez-like hats: like a low-budget version of the Buckingham Palace Guard. The estate was one of Tito's many residences built in the Cold War early-'60s style familiar to anyone who's seen a James Bond film or visited the UN. There are, of course, no red stars, but there is one bust of Tito placed alone and unattended in the foyer.

Through security, we enter the main hall, "where many heads of state were entertained," I'm told. It boasts a parquet floor, one baby grand piano, 18-foot ceilings, and a plush carpet the entire 54-foot length of the hall. A small reception table now holds a compact make-up kit for the President's TV appearance.

A flurry of aides and the ubiquitous security men mill around for an hour before he makes his appearance. Most, except the security, begin to get the breathless jitters one sees in underlings forever concerned about their jobs.

And then Franjo Tudjman enters, relaxed and smiling wearily at the make-up lady, comically annoyed at having to undergo another TV interview. He is a man of 76, with a rigid back and expressive hands. He speaks without once unclenching his teeth, and always through the right side of his mouth, somewhere between a stroke victim and W.C. Fields.

His emotions are all on the surface. He is passionate about his country, and short-tempered with all criticism. He is a man completely made of politics. To every question, personal or political, he answers in terms of historical forces and allegiances: fascism, communism, and everything and everybody in between who may be the enemy of Croatian nationalism. It's a familiar rap to anyone acquainted with his beliefs, and one that informs every single action since his run for the presidency. Other opinions and facts are simply not addressed or acknowledged. It's a single-mindedness befitting a military man, but questionable for a head of state.

Only the day before this interview, October 6, 1997, a deal is announced in which 10 Bosnian Croat war crimes suspects "voluntarily" surrender to The Hague. This announcement is followed by the release of a $40 million credit to Croatia by the International Monetary Fund, an amount much less than my literary advance.

I decide to test his anger with a few of the questions.

"Mr. President, yesterday Croatia agreed that its war criminals will surrender themselves to The Hague. Do you see war crimes as an unavoidable part of war? It was reported that when you learned about the death camps in Bosnia in 1993 you expressed no surprise, saying that others had camps as well."

He grimaces: is it the blinding TV lights or anger toward my question?

"I do not think it would be correct to speak about a people who voluntarily go to The Hague Tribunal as war criminals," he speaks through his interpreter, "because according to any national or international law – they have been indicted, but nobody is guilty until proven so." Tudjman pauses. Moments later the interpreter pauses. I start to ask a follow-up, when Tudjman continues. "I definitely am in favor and support investigation of all such cases, but again, let me repeat, I am not in favor of regarding in the same terms those who caused the aggression, who caused all these tragedies, who jeopardized both the existence of Croatia and the life of its citizens, and those people who during various operations could not curb, could not control their feelings of revenge, their wishes to retaliate."

The tone of his response is filled with such finality that I wonder if our interview is over before it even begins.

I plow on with my next question. "Mr. President, there are critics who claim your political party has replaced the communists as a one-party regime, in which your appointees dominate the economy, and in which the main media are under strict control."

He bows his head, laughs, then, responds, as if placating a baby who had wet the carpet. "Well, I know that you are well intentioned, so I will try to answer some of these questions. First of all, let me claim that there are more democratic rights being granted in this country that in any Western country." He coughs, swallows, and continues like a patient with a bad taste of medicine on his tongue. "And I can also claim with full responsibility that I personally, and the Croatian government, have less influence, less impact on TV, than is the case in your own country, the United States."

"But when I spoke recently with Mate Granic, your foreign minister, he told me, off the record, that your government 'quite frankly has more control of the TV media than the press.'"

In that split second, Tudjman turns angry, huffing and shrugging his shoulders like a turkey in a cockfight.

"Mate, Mate, Mate ..." Although his foreign minister is not in the room, I can only imagine how he now feels the cold hands of Tudjman slapping his face in disapproval. Then Tudjman falls silent.

"Mr. President, is that the end of our interview?"

That is the end of our interview.

He leaves immediately. Seconds after he's gone, the entire crew has a good laugh, and everyone is grabbing heavy drinks from the kitchen. It is 11:30 a.m. They're imagining how the old man will chew out Mate Granic, this poor, liberal cabinet official – the Little Monk, as he is nicknamed – who was once considered to be next in line when Tudjman dies. I hope I didn't just change the course of international politics. I'd better book my return ticket.

Chapter Eight

"Some of My Best Friends Are War Criminals"

> "Nationalism is the final stage of Communism."
> – Adam Michnik

I walk into a cramped but impossibly tidy office to meet my first soon-to-be-indicted war-crime suspect, Croatian Army General Janko Bobetko. Short, round, ingratiatingly gruff, impossibly vainglorious, he has a stern and absolutist persona that does hand-to-hand combat with his overwhelming lavender cologne.

Because he has kept me waiting, I jump in with my most direct question first: "Did Tudjman speak with Milosevic about dividing Bosnia?"

"Your question is like asking the accused to prove that he's not guilty."

Why is everyone here so touchy?

"The President says that he never discussed a division of Bosnia with Milosevic," he says. "And there is no evidence to prove that he did. You want me to prove that I'm not guilty. This is like what happened in Russia where 22 million people were killed based on this kind of argument."

We discuss how Tudjman pushed back the US pressure for him to forge a strong, formal alliance with the Bosnian Muslims, and whether this was Tudjman's stalling strategy to unite his territorial gains.

With cologne wafting in my nostrils I recall how US diplomat Richard Holbrooke, another boundless package of energy and ego, explained it to me: "When the two sides began fighting each other over recaptured territory, it was our worst nightmare come true. Negotiations broke down. There was an amazing scene when we went into Tudjman's palace. Tudjman started yelling at Izetbegovic, 'We have suffered the casualties, and we liberated 80 percent of this territory ourselves. You've done nothing. Now you demand we turn over to you towns that belong to Croatia – that Croatians freed? You insist we capture areas and then turn them over to you. This is simply unacceptable.' Izetbegovic just shrunk back and said nothing. He could have said, 'You never gave us any arms,' but he didn't."

The general takes in my question, sips his espresso, and answers: "Tudjman had to find a way out to stop the war with the Muslims. By Muslims sending in *mujahideen*, a bloody conflict sided against the Croats. Today, certainly it is clear that Tudjman was in an impossible situation. It calls for special analysis."

He then hands me a hardbound copy of his newly published book and tells me that everything I need to know is in there.

The book is entirely in Croatian.

"Thank you," I say.

He autographs it, and hands it to me again, as if sealing a deal. "That will be fifty dollars," he says.

* * *

One night in Zagreb I speak with George long distance, and again hear how deeply he values power and the power players, and why he continually discourages my interviews with the opposition in Croatia, one by one: "He's marginalized ... He's out of the mainstream ... He's an old Partisan living in the past ..."

Were Tudjman's designs on Bosnia really a security concern, as George insists? Or, as his critics claim, was Tudjman's goal to create an ethnically pure, religiously sacrosanct "Greater Croatia"? I have to find out for myself.

This motivation leads me to the most intriguing character I meet in the Balkans, my own Deep Throat insider, who I call the Priest.

Chapter Nine

"The Smoking Guns"

> "I love my country too much to be a nationalist."
> **– Albert Camus**

The Priest is one of the top twelve people in the Bosnian Croat Federation and is undergoing a spiritual or, as he puts it, "existential" crisis. During the war he is close to the Last Loyal Soldier, Mate Boban, the head of Bosnia-Herzegovina's Croatian ruling party, and the man who, had he not died, would surely have been the most wanted Croat war criminal in the world.

'The Priest' is the name I choose to describe the man's shattered faith in God and Croatia, and his corrupted belief in democracy and the human spirit: another legacy of the war. The Priest is as sophisticated as Tudjman is simple, as questioning as Tudjman is doubtless, as disaffected as Tudjman is devout. Through George's introduction, I meet the Priest at a café hidden behind the main square in Zagreb. He chain-smokes – measured, fastidious – and relates how he lost three secretaries to sniper fire in his office, "their heads exploded as they fell to my feet …" He casts his eyes down. "War is horrible. Horrible. And it's harder to get back from it as a sane person. Therefore I think that all of us – all of us – should be eliminated – at least for some time, till first we recuperate ourselves to see who is willing to come back. But I have seen very few good people, if I may say so, very few good people.

"One of them who was definitely good was little Georgie – little Georgie — young Georgie and friends who came from US and Canada. All of them idealists, and enthusiastically trying to assist, trying to show a right path, but no one was listening, actually. No one was listening ..."

The Priest's complaint targets an obstinate Tudjman and his regime's tight control over the Croats in Bosnia. The Priest is also one of many who claim that Tudjman cut a deal with the Serbian President Slobodan Milosevic to divide Bosnia between them. This is the story I read and hear about over and over again, as the most recently told conspiracy theory in the Balkans and one vehemently denied by Tudjman (who sued a human rights activist in Zagreb for accusing Tudjman about it in print).

The division of Bosnia was a negotiation item in almost all talks among the political leaders of ex-Yugo, as well as the international peace envoys. As George is fond of reminding me: "Look, Joe, this is politics. All sides negotiate with their enemies, this happens all the time, throughout all history. How can you have diplomacy unless you keep the links open with your enemy?"

In late 1991, under the leadership of Tudjman, Mate Boban, aka "the Mobster," creates the Croat Union of "Herzeg-Bosna," an autonomous region in Bosnia-Herzegovina with its own police, army, currency, and education, where most of its population is Croat. By mid-'92, it comes into conflict in districts with Muslim majorities, with atrocities committed by Croat militia.

In April of 1993, Croat forces launch a coordinated attack against Muslim civilians in nine Bosnian villages. Most of the victims are elderly people, women, children, and infants, including several who are burned alive. Years later, the International Criminal Tribunal for the former Yugoslavia affirms there was no military justification for the attacks.

The Priest claims that he has in his possession documents that link Tudjman directly to these war crimes. Goldmine, I think.

"When can I see the documents?" I ask, straining to contain my saliva. But the Priest brushes off the request, saying that in time he will provide them, and ends the first of our meetings.

That leaves me with only opinions with which to paint Tudjman's portrait. I have decided this is not an option. The consequences of the alternative, however, I am woefully unprepared for.

Chapter Ten

"Enemy of the State"

> "A shady lane breeds mud."
> – **Hopi proverb**

"No, no, no, Joe—"

I've never seen Jakov this upset.

"Yes, yes, Jakov, I want to go to Sarajevo."

"No, no, Joe, you can't."

"What do you mean? There's a flight every day. Just book it for me."

"No, Joe, I cannot."

"That's ridiculous. You hired a car to drive me all the way from Zagreb to Ljubljana. Just book the flight."

"A bomb exploded there yesterday in front of church. I cannot let you."

"I know, but I need to go there. It's where the story's taking me. I'll make arrangements with your travel agent."

"Impossible!" he says.

During the entire trip he has paid for everything: hotels, room service, phone, fax, dry cleaning. But at the mere mention of Sarajevo, he freezes.

Well, Jakov will have to find someone else to parade in front of his mass graves. There's another side to this story: it wasn't just the Serbs who committed war crimes. I would find the guilty parties. And in Bosnia, Jakov would have no way to monitor me. No more scheduled interviews, no more history lectures, and no more black sedans trailing me everywhere I go. I'd be a free agent – out of reach of the Zagreb government.

I need to get there – Bosnia is at the heart of Tudjman's story. And in Sarajevo, I knew I would find my answer.

Through Ivo I meet Damir, the cocky, clean-shaven, and slightly demented operator of the only opposition radio station in Zagreb. Damir says he can find me a cheap flight to Sarajevo. But first – drinks, dinner, and yet more drinks, watching satellite TV from his home, flipping between Croatian porn and Serbian sit-coms – and it's really hard to tell the difference after a bottle of *slivovitz*.

I pass out. I'm in a fever dream. In it, I see a bearded Croat bearing gifts: a case of cheap plum brandy, a bag of pot, four vials of heroin, and a sack of secondhand AK-47s.

Damir's friend has arrived, in the mood for fun.

"Okay, Joe," shouts Damir. "Now we have real party!"

"I don't know, Damir. I just want a ticket to Sarajevo."

"We have ticket here, and now we have party because tomorrow you fly to Muslim shithole! *Zivjeli!*"

We drink.

Now we're in his jeep, going I-don't-know-where, and going there real fast. Our party of three arrives in the dead of night at what looks like a military garrison.

"Damir, what the fuck are we doing here?"

"Ssshhhh!" He points into the distance.

We're out of the jeep now, and begin to creep up a small hill, slipping and falling in the mud, until we make it to a barbed wire fence. Next thing I know, Damir and the drug dealer are cutting into the fence and dragging me under it. We run up to a wooden shed, and the dealer takes out an axe and starts whacking at it. I'm sweating bullets, Damir hands me an empty sack, and they start filling it with ammunition from the shed.

Finally, the lone guard in his post at the end of the road wakes up from the racket. He begins running toward us, then stops and starts firing his rifle!

POW! POW! POW!

My heart is beating out of my chest as we run back to the jeep, jump in, and take off. The Croats are laughing like maniacs, and I start laying into Damir.

"Do you have a fucking death wish, or are you just trying to kill me?"

Damir's smoking a cigarette, like we've just finished a stroll in the park. "Thank you, Joe; you are now one of us. This regime has got too many crooks; all stole from Croatians, and all their friends are war criminals. I've had my radio station broken into sixteen times, I've had to raise thousands of dollars in new license fees, every month a new one. They want us to die because we call them who they are – crooks. We want only to be ready when they decide to come after us – with guns."

It's dawn when we start driving to the airport. The dealer is now jabbering at me from the back seat. After a minute, I turn to Damir, who translates: "He says he wrote screenplay about a little red mouse who carries Uzi. Can you get him meeting with DreamWorks?"

I finally awake, but I'm still at Damir's filthy apartment. No bearded friend, no drugs, no guns. Reality and paranoia have finally blurred; the first sign of the dreaded Balkan Bug.

When I eventually check into the airport, I'm somehow muddy and unshaved, cigarette and whiskey fumes rising from me like smoke from a torched building. I fear my trip to Bosnia will bring more failure and more delusion, and no possible cure for the Bug, until a familiar voice calls me.

"Joe?"

It's the Priest, and he's on the same flight. I practically shout for joy at seeing him, but he motions me to keep my voice down. He leads me to the VIP lounge, and only then converses, in hushed tones.

"How fortuitous we are on the same flight, Joe. Of course, once we land we must separate. Only government employees and the Croatian Mafia take this flight."

The Croatian Mafia: the happy gang of criminals doing the dirty work of the Croatian government. The Priest seems to know a lot about the Croatian Mafia – a little too much, perhaps.

We are two of only three passengers on the plane. Nevertheless, midway through the flight he asks me to move to the rear. And when we land, he says, I should wait five minutes after he's exited before I leave the plane.

I have no clue whether I enjoy his confidence or am just being manipulated. But I know one thing: I'm not leaving until I unravel the truth inside the Balkan onion.

I spend the rest of the flight in silence, and when we finally land, I'm actually happy to see the decimated airport.

Chapter Eleven

"Bombs Can't Stop the Drink"

"What's the difference between the Croatian Mafia and
the Italian Mafia?
In Italy the Mafia is still illegal."
– Joke told by Stipe Mesic, Croatia's Second President

Sarajevo International Airport, October 1997: A portable military control tower sits on the tarmac, a lonely guardian on what was the front line of the war in Bosnia. During the war, the airport became a sitting duck for Serb artillery from all sides in the adjacent mountains. Surrounding the runway now are rows upon rows of modest two-story houses without roofs, their dark sockets leading to empty wooden shells. In between these ghost structures, three or four families have set up homes, with laundry strung across the tiny terraces, and a TV satellite dish angled outward. It is two years after the war, and Sarajevo has had its spirit drained. It is a ghost town without ghosts.

The road from the airport is the notorious Sniper Alley, a short jaunt smack-dab in the middle of former Serb artillery, a road where luckless pedestrians were killed daily. It is only a few kilometers long. A colorful building stands empty, racked with pockmarks and holes of war: a former pensioner's home.

The Serbs, I was told by the Priest, are blackmailing the new Bosnian central government by preventing sufficient supply of Russian gas to enter. Heating systems are thus seriously devastated. Devastation: the word most used to describe Sarajevo. By November, a leaked report by the executive body of the European Union would detail the wholesale loss to the Bosnian government of tens of millions of dollars, mostly from black market and other criminal trade, by all three ethnic groups. The city's infrastructure is at a virtual standstill; electricity and the trams are running, but very little else has been rebuilt. The view outside the world's most famous Holiday Inn is a typical testament: a twenty-story building with almost its entire facade blown away; nothing but iron girders and cement remain.

Alone in my hotel room at the Holiday Inn, I notice a piece of carpet that has come undone, revealing a recent bullet hole. I stare at it as I replay the audiotapes from my interview with the Priest:

"In 1992, I was in Sarajevo, in Ministry of Foreign Affairs, a prime figure; I could do everything. And Bosnian Prime Minister, Haris Silajdic, was calling me every day: 'Why don't you involve your people in diplomacy? Why don't they help us, your Muslim neighbors? Our people are being slaughtered. We can work together to fight the Serbs, etc., etc." A pause as he drags from his cigarette. "My hands were tied."

"Why was that?"

"The Zagreb government prevented us from doing so."

"Are you saying that Tudjman's Bosnia policy was to fight the Muslims – even at the time when Croats and Muslims finally joined forces against the Serbs?"

"Your friend the President—"

"Tudjman's not my friend."

"Of course. Well, he never understood Muslims, never lived with them as we did in Sarajevo."

"Does that explain his designs on Bosnia to partition it? Were his plans just a land grab, to claim much of Bosnia for Croatia?"

"As you say so."

"And Mate Boban was the man who implemented Tudjman's plan?"

"Boban was much too complex a character. He took Muslim refugees into his own home during the height of the war when chaos reigned; when Serbs, Muslims, and Croats all fought each other."

"But Boban set up the death camps in Bosnia."

"It was at the behest of your friend, the President. I have a huge documentation about what was happening. I have kept letters, for my own protection."

"You have signed orders from Tudjman to Boban about the camps?"

"The problem with Boban was his total devotion to Tudjman. That was faith; that was belief; that was incredible trust in the President. Boban was an ultimate servant, if I may say so; the ultimate servant and the last loyal soldier. That was his disaster, of course – he never objected.

"And when the pressure on Tudjman to disband the camps became too great, Tudjman relieved Boban of his post. At the end, Boban was turned to major enemy – and major scapegoat for Tudjman."

The facts I am turning up make me edgy: to paint the complete picture of Tudjman the man without lauding him or vilifying him means I can please no one. Jakov won't like the critical parts of the book (although I had warned him), while the majority of the Western press will think it is a rehabilitation job done by a hired hack/Croatian mouthpiece (and non-historian to boot). In former Yugo, taking a middle-road position doesn't win you any friends either; it reminds too many of Tito's non-aligned policy. As the Balkan psychology goes, you are either with us or against us. In some cases you either take sides, or are put aside.

It is not necessarily true that the Balkans automatically breed violence – any more than a recently divorced man automatically becomes a rutting dog; this is something I would have almost believed – if it hadn't been for my newly acquired habit of falling in love with every other woman I meet. A habit that, combined with a US passport, could land you in trouble in any country, but particularly in the Balkans.

I convince myself that there is no grand effort to shield me from Tudjman's critics or spoon-feed me propaganda or bribe my loyalty when, night after night, not one single prostitute is ever sent to my hotel room. But the stories of midnight phone threats and car bombs do make me cautious. What if they don't like what I write? The dogged journalist in me tells me to keep digging, but I also keep looking over my shoulder.

* * *

Tudjman saw in Bosnia his chance to reclaim ancient Croatian territory, not simply to secure a buffer zone to protect Dalmatia. And he used the Bosnian Croats as his proxy, not wanting to risk Croatia for Bosnia. His goal, which he inherited from his father, never changed: to get a highly homogeneous, expanded Croatia under Zagreb's control. As Richard Holbrooke tells me: "During the worst fighting in Bosnia, '93-'94, when Boban was directing offensives against the Muslims, Tudjman could have stopped the war; but because it fit into his goal of a mini-state, he let it continue." To fulfill this dream he recruited Boban, his devout, loyal servant.

"He was a blowhard," recalls Peter Galbraith about Boban. "I met him in July of 1993 ... And I listened to him for about an hour go on about the Muslims and their evils, and then I said, 'Now I'm going to tell you something. It is utterly unacceptable to use food as a weapon' – because they were holding up convoys – 'we cannot tolerate holding prisoners in inhumane conditions ...' And he was really taken aback. And so he promised he'd try to do something about the convoys and the prisoners. The next day he called me, said they were going to release the prisoners. And, in fact, over the ensuing days they released more than four thousand prisoners ... As was typical in this war, Boban's wonderful promises disappeared after some weeks, and the Bosnian Croats began again to block the convoys. At that point I realized that the only way to deal with Boban was to get rid of him."

According to Galbraith, he and US Special Envoy to the peace talks, Charles Redman, worked over Tudjman with a carrot and a stick: join with the Bosnian Muslims in an alliance and "the door to the west would be open to Croatia," or face sanctions by the UN Security Council. Tudjman finally agreed, and sent his Little Monk Mate Granic to the peace talks in Bosnia to negotiate the Washington Agreement, which would merge the Bosnian Croat and Muslim armies.

The Croatian Bosnian military, however, threatened to scuttle the emerging agreement, so Galbraith saw his chance to eliminate Mate Boban, the Mobster, from the scene. During a late 1993 BBC interview, Galbraith linked Mate Boban to the atrocities committed by the Croats in Bosnia – stopping just short of calling him a war criminal. The interview got a lot of play in the tightly controlled Croatian press. "To me," says Galbraith, "it was a signal as to what was coming."

* * *

Zeljko Olujic was one of Tudjman's defense lawyers in the early '80s, when Tudjman was indicted after speaking to the foreign press.

Olujic is the lead lawyer defending the indicted Croat war crime suspects in The Hague when we meet in the swanky bar at Zagreb's Hotel International. He is of dark complexion, tall and swaggering, with a reputation as a lady killer (figuratively, as far as I know). He claims, much like Tudjman, that it is unfair to indict these Croats, since Serbia was the aggressor in the war and Croatia the victim.

It is a polite, urbane discussion, until I say: "But the Geneva Convention of 1949 – Articles 146 and 147 – do not make distinctions in who commits war crimes. It seems you have no legal precedent for your statement."

"Yes," Olujic nods, now impatient, "but America is trying to match the same number of Croat indictments as Serb indictments. And that's because America wants to forget the mistake they made at the beginning of 1990 for not stopping the war."

Of course, I should have known that it was our fault.

Chapter Twelve

"War, What War?"

> "The end move in politics is always to pick up a gun."
> – R. Buckminster Fuller

The Priest takes the crucifix down from the wall and carefully, deliberately, delicately places it inside a drawer. He removes the paintings of Christ and the photographs of the Pope, wraps them in dirty newspapers, and packs them away. He vows never to unwrap them for as long as he lives.

The Priest remembers the Mobster fondly, recalling that Boban was "too honest … in a way too sincere." Whenever Galbraith reprimands him about the Croatian atrocities, Boban fires off a litany of recent Muslim atrocities, then reminisces about the time he saw his first photograph of a Vietnamese girl burned by American napalm. The Priest chuckles at the memory.

He claims that, throughout the war, the Mobster sheltered 25 or 30 Muslim refugees in his mother's house. In Boban's defense, the Priest says that the Mobster was overwhelmed by the simultaneous fight against the Serbs and the Muslims. And now that Croatia's entrance to the West is being shepherded by the United States government, now that Tudjman is about to see his life's ambition realized before the ink is even set to the history books, and long after Ambassador Galbraith targets Boban for international crucifixion, the Mobster has suddenly outlived his political usefulness. He is dismissed from his post by Tudjman, and replaced by the less disagreeable, if impermeably boring, Kresimir Zubak.

The Priest concedes that Boban was not up to the task of Zagreb's directives, and was never able to organize or control the tiny fiefdoms and mini-mafias dispersed throughout Bosnia. "Mate Boban is generally perceived as equal to Radovan Karadzic," he says, his eyes downcast and distant, "but Boban was something very different from the public picture of him. Boban was very humble, very modest. He was always with his soldiers, eating the same food they were eating. He was being pretty stubborn, unwilling to listen to other advice, other than Mr. Tudjman … He did the dirty work for Tudjman, and at the end, Boban became just a toy in his hand. He was turned into – due to Zagreb's wrong policy in regard to Muslims – a major enemy."

The Mobster perishes like William Casey, dying from a brain aneurysm. But, unlike the American spymaster, Boban dies without secrets, or at least hidden agendas. It is out in the open: his uncompromising and genocidal assaults in the name of his homeland, and his unshakable loyalty, even to the end, when his savior abandons him.

The Priest boards a plane in Sarajevo, his briefcase neat and tidy with executive orders, and scans the shell-shocked city that once held kind memories, long ago. A fog has settled, touching the hem of his coat. The fog used to mean the people's only safety from constant sniper fire. Now, blanketing the city, it threatens to erase it completely; the people's past and future shrouded in collective denial and neglect.

Boban's devotion cannot be questioned, nor can the demands from Tudjman to his last loyal soldier. Years after their deaths, conclusive proof surfaces of their plans for the annexation of Bosnia-Herzegovina, the creation of "Greater Croatia," and the cover-up of war crimes.

The Priest is speaking to himself now: "The Muslims were considered a most prominent place in the Croatian nation, until now," he reflects. "But it is inevitable that relationships between Croatia and Muslims will improve. We had no problems with the Muslims throughout the twentieth century in Yugoslavia. A pity; but, to be cynical, at the end, the war came to be fruitful for both nations to recognize the rights of each other."

∗ ∗ ∗

Though I never secure the Priest's alleged documents, it does become clear to me how many resources the Croatian government is deploying into keeping Tudjman from being called to the International War Crimes Tribunal. The deal Croatia made with the IMF to release the $40 Million credit in exchange for sending ten Bosnian Croat war crimes suspects to The Hague is so obvious even I can understand it. True to his Mafia-like instincts, for their loyalty Tudjman provided monetary and other support to the suspects and their families.

It's also clear that I can't convince Jadranka to fly with me to Sarajevo, let alone make love. So, once in Bosnia, I hire a female interpreter, and invite her to dinner.

Chapter Thirteen

"War Crimes and Miss Demeanors"

> "If you can't convince them, confuse them."
> – Harry S. Truman

The office of the President of the Bosnian Croats is microscopic compared to the foyer of Tudjman's palace, and Kresimir Zubak is just the man to be outsized by his own tiny workspace, however posh and polished. He walks an impressively fine tightrope, balancing his subservience to Tudjman, his ultimate boss, with the ownership of his own barely distinguishable policy initiatives.

During my interview I find myself staring at Aida's perfectly shaped Bosnian lips, then into her sad, scared eyes. With each bout of translation, Zubak's presence recedes into the room; his boring litany of ancient disputes becomes an instant memory. I am interviewing a wind-up toy, but sitting next to a living doll.

"So, you American writer, you come to Sarajevo with thought we are all fundamentalists," Aida scolds me at lunch after my interview.

"Not at all: You're all very urbane, very cool."

Sarajevo, Bosnia's capital, always had a reputation, deserved or not, of being the region's model of multiculturalism. The Sarajevans pride themselves on their Western-like urbanity. Throughout the years when the war nearly destroyed everything in their city, the people displayed resilience, optimism, and humor. "Come back Tito," reads graffiti scrawled across a building, "All is forgiven." Beneath it, a tart response, from the mouth of a cartoon drawing of Tito: "You've got to be kidding!"

Aida tells me how she would defiantly put on make-up, blue eye shadow and red lipstick, and proudly walk down the streets of Sarajevo. "I wanted to taunt the snipers," she explains, "to say to them: 'I am wearing Lancôme, and you can just wear your leaves and mud.'

"My mother stayed at home for entire war. And one day a piece of mortar hit her; it had ricocheted off a building, and hurt her leg. She is fine now, but she has never left her home. You didn't know whether to go out or stay inside; either could mean the end of your life, yet you had to find food, water, and to try to live your life."

Now, with the trams running and electricity working most of the time, Sarajevans are back on the streets, proving once again that they would not choose between living on their knees or dying on their feet – they would rather be drinking in the cafés.

"And you, Joe. Are you married?"

"No, but I used to be. I was married for 13 years until my divorce."

"Oh. And how many children?"

"I don't have any."

"No children? No, that cannot be."

"No, no kids."

She shakes her head, and says, "You wasted 13 years of your life. Excuse me, I'm sorry, but you did."

"Well, I don't exactly see it that way."

"Look at Ali here."

We turn and watch her three-year-old throw sugar across the Holiday Inn lobby. He screams in joy, then trots over and rubs his cute, sticky face into mine.

"He likes you. She glances at me with mischievous hope. "He needs a visa."

* * *

"Hello, Joe. Watcha gonna do?"

The phone connection is scratchy, but I distinctly recognize the sweet-and-sour voice. "Hi Jadranka."

"You are enjoying Sarajevo?

"Yes."

"Joe?"

"Yes?"

"I miss you. When are you coming back to Zagreb?"

"I thought you didn't think of me that way. Don't confuse me."

"Well, I didn't think so either, until you left. Now, my darling, I miss you, and – when will you come to see me?"

"I don't know. I'm flying straight out of Sarajevo to Vienna, then to New York."

"Then, my darling, I will come to New York ... Joe?"

"Yes, I'm still here."

"You won't change your address on me, will you?"

In the Balkans, they're always one step ahead.

* * *

"Club Jez," she tells the cab driver, who speeds off down Sniper Alley as though the war's still raging.

Aida's hand is on Ali, who fiddles with the back-door window, then the handle. It snaps open and the cold air hits us. I lunge for the child and catch him by the collar. The door is swinging wildly now, as the driver negotiates a turn with the aplomb of a drunken teen.

"Look out!" My call of alarm is batted off like Ali's own yelps of glee.

"Oh, don't worry." Aida shuts the door. For her it's a small annoyance, like wiping up snot from his nose. Or mine.

At the café, she uses a scattershot, double-barreled technique. Hence, chances are good she'll hit one of my buttons.

"So why are you scared of me?"

"I'm not scared of you."

"You are afraid I will steal your money."

"No, of course not. I'm on a limited budget, that's all. They didn't even want me to come to Bosnia."

"I think you need to have family."

"I have a family, back home."

"You told me you didn't have kids. You are lying?"

"No, I'm not. I don't have kids, I—"

"You need kids. Everyone needs a family. Buy me another double scotch."

We close the café, and head back to the Holiday Inn via Sniper Alley, where, just three years ago, Aida was shot in the shoulder by a Bosnian Serb sniper when she was five months pregnant with Ali.

I don't see myself as some Hollywood actor portraying the Great White Savior of a war-besieged people; this isn't war time anymore; I don't need to save a soul; I'm not the guilty one – so, what is this gnawing inside my gut?

The cab drops her and little Ali in front of their home, nestled safely beside the police station behind the hotel. Her mother would be sleeping now. For two years, since the American-engineered Dayton Peace Accord, the city has been able to sleep. No mortar fragments will fly in through the window and wound her mother again – as long as NATO remains on the ground.

Chapter Fourteen

"And the Winner Is"

> "A divorce is like an amputation: you survive it,
> but there's less of you."
> **– Margaret Atwood**

August 28, 1995: Another mortar hits the Sarajevo market, killing 38 people this time. President Clinton presses NATO into running bombing raids against Serbian military targets. After 16 days, this bombing campaign finally pushes the Serbs to negotiate a settlement.

Like a teacher chastising a group of schoolyard bullies, Secretary of State Warren Christopher forces Tudjman, Milosevic, and Izetbegovic to rise and shake hands. Thus beginning the "proximity talks" at an air force base in Dayton Ohio, which the US was brokering under the strong hand of Assistant Secretary of State Richard Holbrooke. Nicknamed "Raging Bull," Holbrooke's hands-on style affronts many in the State Department, but proves effective in negotiations.

"Franjo Tudjman is the key to Dayton," Holbrooke emphasizes to me.

Tudjman entered Dayton with all the chips, and collected even more. He spent considerable time alone with his old horse-trading buddy Slobodan Milosevic. Franjo and Slobo, who are on a first-name basis, cut a number of land deals, including one called the Erdut Agreement that hands over Serb-controlled territory to Croatia.

Within three weeks the Dayton Peace Accord was reached. The agreement, which has been called the most expensive ceasefire in history, has kept the peace since '95. This is the peace that now keeps Aida and her mother safe.

I should thank Franjo Tudjman for being that key to peace. He wagered his country and his people on his vision of an expanded Croatia, and was able to build a credible army almost overnight. By bullying and manipulating his Bosnian Croats he was able to co-opt them, and use the Croat-Muslim alliance to fend off the Serbs. He also kept the Muslims at bay and unbalanced through his close negotiations with Milosevic. And he garnered respect – of sorts – from the international community. Certainly they used him to broker a long-delayed peace from the hell of an ultimately avoidable war. And he placated their human rights demands by sacrificing Boban. Even while I denounce his goals, I thank Tudjman. Tito himself would have been impressed.

Yet the old Yugoslavia is now ethnically cleansed, with half of the Serb population gone from Croatia, and "Brotherhood and Unity," that old Partisan slogan, a faded memory in outdated textbooks. Tito, who had been so successful in keeping the virus of nationalism from infecting his ethnic groups, would also have been saddened and afraid. The new Yugoslavs are celebrating their ethnic, religious and geographic differences, not their similarities. After four years of virulent fighting, terror, mass graves, detention camps, torture, rape, wholesale destruction of homes and villages, and the flight of millions of refugees, the people of ex-Yugoslavia have learned to hate once again. Reconciliation and repatriation are more than a challenge for those left alive.

* * *

On a drizzly, chilly Sunday morning, I pass the sidewalk stores on the cobbled streets of Sarajevo. Artists have painted the walkways with Sarajevan roses: splashes of red, marking, like police chalk outlines, deaths by snipers.

I turn a corner and come upon a small crowd gathered in front of a mosque. At first it seems like a wedding, or a funeral. But as I get closer, I notice the insignia of the Bosnian Muslim extremist party. This is a political gathering in a religious setting – very Balkan. And, also very Balkan, the Muslims are pushing their own ethnic exclusionary agenda.

These are the same extremists whose *mujahideen* soldiers committed their own share of atrocities against Serbs and Croats in Bosnia. They are connected to murder, rape, brutal mistreatment, and one barbaric ritual beheading.

As I get closer to the mosque, the security guards with their semi-automatics start getting twitchy. Most of them know all the players in town: who are with the UN, who are the reporters, who are the profiteers – but they don't know me. I look like a lost tourist, which of course I am. But I am definitely not welcome. One guard looks like he's seen it all and stares at me as if he could take me out with as much effort as swatting a fly. Another is young and red-faced, only too eager to prove his mettle.

Word filters back to the Holiday Inn; when I return, my room is suddenly in demand, and I'm asked politely to vacate. Obviously, I have overstayed my visit.

To date I still don't believe it was my trip to the mosque that got me evicted, although it got me noticed. No, they discovered the real reason for my visit – the reason I was hired: to rehabilitate Tudjman's image, and keep him out of The Hague.

During this time period, it is later revealed, Croatian Military Intelligence was running a counterintelligence campaign named

"Operation Hague" to protect indictees and subvert investigations. ICTY prosecutors were placed under surveillance, evidence was stolen, and witnesses threatened. My writing assignment was simply a minor initiative in Tudjman's grand scheme to subvert justice.

* * *

"It's because of you that I am leaving." I was feeling playful now, teasing Aida with my feeble jokes.

I take her by the shoulders and push her gently against the bed, daring to nuzzle her neck. That is the closest thing to sex in my entire trip. Even so, in strict Muslim terms, we should now be married.

"No, I can't." She is annoyed, slightly alarmed, and confused. I hadn't planned to do this. All morning I made promises to myself not to come on to her.

I pull back. "I'm sorry. My behavior is not professional." I stand up, walk to my suitcase, and continue packing. "Please forgive me."

"No, it's okay …" Again those sad eyes. "But you are leaving today." She is pulling every string.

"Yes, you know that."

"And you will ask Ambassador in Vienna to get me visa."

"I'll do what I can," I lie; then, like a true American cad, offer to massage her shoulders.

"No, I can't. I am Muslim. I took confession."

"Oh … but you drink."

She just shrugs, smiles, and frets. My plane leaves in an hour. I take her with me to the airport. We sit and have a coffee. My gut is twisting tighter and tighter, my smile is getting weaker and weaker. I buy her a gift – then one for Ali. It's like I'm trying to assuage my guilt as an American for not stopping the war. Or for my not taking sides. She did not take sides. This was not her choice.

Throughout my trip I've been bludgeoned by those I interviewed for not understanding the ancient rivalries, for not intervening soon enough, for not organizing a massive airlift to carry refuges to my New York City apartment. With Aida no bludgeoning was necessary. I managed that myself quite nicely. What she felt for me I do not know: perhaps more than an escape from Sarajevo, and somewhat less than love. Towards the end of my trip it was clear that I was ready to accept any form of affection as an open invitation. It was also clear to those who saw my eyes that I was not ready for any responsibility other than writing this damn book.

What I saw in Aida's eyes that day at the airport was an unfathomable sadness. She told me of Ali's father who went off to war a pumped-up patriot, and who returned changed beyond recognition: an errant, hardened soldier who had committed his share of atrocities. When a family member becomes unfamiliar, the stranger seems more familiar.

"Is that why you come here, American writer?" she asks, letting me hold her warm hand in mine. "To get away from your divorce?"

"I loved someone, once, very much."

"And it was not your wife?"

I shake my head. "No, she wasn't. She was the greatest love of my life and I let her go."

"And you want to punish yourself in Bosnia?"

"I just couldn't stand living a secret life anymore. I felt guilty as hell. And I guess I'm just a coward – letting her slip away like that. It's the biggest mistake I ever made."

"And so, now you run away again."

We share a smile, and my flight is called. I wave goodbye to the two sweetest creatures in Sarajevo and start to board the plane. After one month of travel and interviews, I am leaving the Balkans, with more questions than answers.

I did not see my Balkan trip as an escape to the Foreign Legion. But Aida's words hit their mark. In the last years of my marriage my months-long affair with another woman triggered more than the raging hormones of a teenager. It triggered a tsunami of Catholic guilt, forcing me into a decision I regretted for years. I broke up the affair, confessed to my wife, who confessed her own infidelity. We fooled ourselves into thinking the marriage could be saved, but inevitably separated.

Into the Balkans I carried the grief of my divorce like a hair blanket, and my regret for a love I let go like the most precious baggage I ever owned.

* * *

On the flight back to New York, there is no CIA man smuggling secrets in his shorts, and I am too consumed in thought to notice anything. I work at getting inside Franjo Tudjman the man.

There are two strains in Tudjman's character, both formed in early life, which steer his actions in two directions: the Freedom Fighter Tudjman – the Partisan peasant organizer and enemy of fascism; and the Presidential Tudjman – the leader of the nation, and defender of his race and religion. Both dovetail within the texture of Croatian heritage, and are made explicit in Tudjman's courting of both the hardline nationalists and the Zagreb liberals.

An agile politician, and a visionary, within Tudjman live also the abandoned son, the betrayed patriot, and the besieged warrior. Is his core weakness the same strength that sustained him in jail, that helped carry out his father's dream, that led his army in a battle against the Serbs and his diplomatic corps against the bias of international opinion? In his attempts to "reconcile" the medieval symbols of Croatian statehood, did he fall into the trap set by Serbian and pro-Serbian propaganda that paints all such efforts as Ustasha revivalism? In his driving battle to avenge his father's death, perhaps he gave over part of his control to that bitter urge; the Master General, the leader and ruler of the first independent Croatia, became a subject to this emotional coalition inside, tagging him as one of several Croatian Spring politicians who waged a campaign for democracy motivated by the dark contours of an ex-prisoner's ethic.

* * *

A few weeks after my return to New York, through my ever-expanding network of Balkan contacts, I meet Indira. A tiny young woman from tiny Montenegro, a country squeezed between Serbia, Bosnia, and Albania, Indira used to work in the government offices of Slobodan Milosevic, where she would drive a girlfriend to an ambassador's house for daily assignations, doing her nails in the car while she waited.

"There is a name for people who do that," she explains when I tell her of my misadventures with the women of the former Yugoslavia. "They are the foreigners who visit battle-worn countries looking for cheap thrills; whichever way the wind blows they go. They are called 'windfuckers.'"

"And is there a name for the women who attach themselves to these foreign men?"

"Yes," she declares: "sluts."

It's no surprise to me that, six months later, Indira marries

Ivo. Together they form RACOON (Reconciliation and Culture Cooperative Network) a New York-based center that provides aid and counseling for Balkan refugees, including survivors of rape and torture. They also give birth to an adorable little boy.

∗ ∗ ∗

With my deadline approaching and the Bug still in my brain, I fall asleep. There is a terrible commotion outside my door, and almost before I can open my eyes, five giant skinhead Croats in dark suits surround me, hog-tie me, beat me senseless, and drag me into their black Mercedes. I look closely at my nearly completed manuscript upon awakening, wondering what inflammatory sentence could have caused this nightmare.

I gaze down on a bundle of brightly colored fabric in my arms. It unwraps and reveals a baby, a cute face gurgling in delight. Its other head, however, is deformed beyond recognition; two dark and caked sockets where the eyes should be. As I relate this dream to Indira, I realize that the infant represents my own ambivalence to my misshapen book, a writer's deepest fear made flesh.

"What is your American expression? Lie down with dogs and put up against fleas," Indira chuckles.

"Thank you; that's a very kind thought."

"I think a book about Tudjman is unnecessary; any book about any of those leaders. This is what I told reporter from *Financial Times*: everybody is interested in power play and backroom deal, but no one remembers people: People who fought, people who suffered, people who died. That is story should be written."

We should all be minorities, we should all intermingle, the races should all intermarry; this should be mandatory. We should become the large extended family we thought we never had; the one, I now know, I could never have; until, that is, I do something of worth, leave something of value behind; a salve, a story, or simply the truth.

The truth, I first thought after landing in the Balkans, is hard to find. But soon I realize that the truth, the naked, unhidden, unashamed truth, is what you do, whom you love, whom you betray. In my haste, I zoom past the truth and crash again in my own land of alienation. One small victory is my remorse beyond fear.

* * *

"Joe!"

"Hi, Jakov."

He is calling some months before my impending deadline, but has never asked to see any early drafts.

"Joe, I just got call from Zagreb. They – somehow they got first hundred pages of your manuscript."

"What?"

"Joe, how did they get it? I don't know."

"Jakov, the only person who has a copy is George Rudman, my researcher."

"I don't know. Who is this George?"

Did he really not know George? "Maybe he showed it to Miles at the UN."

"Joe, Zagreb says 'how can this be biography, it says critical things about Tudjman.'"

"Oh." This is where I start checking the locks on my door.

"I told them, Joe, it's impossible. It has only facts in book."

"Well, I'm going to call George and find out what's happening."

"Please, Joe, just to keep the manuscript between you and me."

Vitomir Miles Raguz is a buddy of George who worked during the war as a member of the Bosnian Croat peace delegation. Some of my sources claim, however, that he also worked as a spy for them. Whatever the truth, Miles is now advisor to the Croatian Mission to the UN, and remains extremely close to George.

George sends an early version of my manuscript to Miles, who then writes a three-page critique, calls me anti-Croat, and chastises me for saying that the Croatian government controls the media – even though it came directly from the lips of their own Prime Minister.

He then sends the memo to Tudjman's office, and other government officials – including some who, like Miles, supported the Mobster.

I call Miles after George confesses to sending him the manuscript.

"Miles, did you speak with George?"

"Yes, this morning. I guess there's some kind of problem?"

"I know that he sent you the manuscript."

"Yeah, I read it. I made some comments, and I passed it on to Zagreb, and—"

"You sent it to Zagreb?"

"Yeah."

"Where in Zagreb?"

"Ah … to the President's office."

"Why was it sent there?"

"Because it deals with the President."

Long pause as images of car bombs explode in my head.

"Miles, this is an unfinished manuscript. And my deal is with Sedlar, not with the UN, not with the Croatian government, and not with the President's office. This has become a very difficult situation now."

"Well, I – uh – I think – it shouldn't be a difficult situation; it could be resolved. The transcript needs lots of work – but there are positive things that can be done to change it."

"I turned this down, you know. There's no way I can write an authorized, glowing book about President Tudjman and have any credibility here in the United States."

"Uh-huh."

"I have total control over the book."

"Uh-huh."

"Now that I've told you this, I trust you will keep this in confidence."

"Right, I got you."

"After all, you gave me an interview, too; and I'm not using your name either."

"Right."

"Joe, I have never pressured you or told you what to write your book." Jakov's words are collegial, but his tone is scolding."

"We both want the same thing, Jakov: a successful book in America that's not just seen as a mouthpiece for the government."

"You know, some people are crazy."

He shows me the cover letter Miles wrote to the President, to Mate Granic, to almost everybody high up in government circles.

"He wasn't supposed to do that, Jakov. I hope this didn't cause any trouble."

"I spoke to top advisor to Tudman, and explained it is unfinished manuscript. It would be like if I had sent all rushes of my film on Stepinac to them."

(He wouldn't have to. Jakov is a known commodity; I'm known as a sci-fi writer.)

"Jakov, they have to understand that in order for the book to have any credibility, it can't avoid areas of controversy."

"Joe, we must put in book about him with Partisans, him with Tito, all areas of controversy. And all true facts. And where there is still no understanding, just say 'we don't know.' Martin Sheen, when we did my film, ask me all the time about this or that, and I send him all information."

"I can go over the manuscript with you right now, if you like."

"No, no, Joe, when it is finished."

I leave his office with one burning question: What did Martin Sheen see in Jakov's glossy brochures that I missed?

Chapter Fifteen

"Home Is Where They Shave"

"Ye shall know the truth, and the truth shall make you mad."
– Aldous Huxley

The emotion boils up in me; I can't contain it. I have to do it. I will do it. I could kiss Miles! I am so happy that they think I am not one of their paid propagandists.

I know what I'm going to do – I'm going to burn the book, and all of the interviews – I don't want to see another trace of it for as long as I live!

The professional in me soon returns after my defiant tantrum. I relent, resume writing, and in a few months complete a 400-page manuscript. One day after I hand it to Jakov, he calls me in.

"Please, Joe, you write very good book, but please to consider make small minor changes."

"Like what?"

"First: the title."

"What's wrong with *In Tito's Shadow*? I think it's very descriptive – of the man, and the country."

"No. Please not to mention anything from old communist time."

"Well, that would make it substantially shorter."

"And please not to mention war crimes."

"I can't do that."

I refuse to make the changes. I'd rather the book go unpublished. Jakov had hoped to co-opt an authentic American voice, to lend the biography more credibility, to make it palatable for Western consumption. Instead, the author bit the hand that fed him.

Jakov, however, is not easily discouraged.

"I have a problem with this," I tell Jakov who is bent forward on the edge of his seat, a towering figure threatening to topple. "If I write the book Eddie wants me to write, and you expect me to write, that would be the end of my career. You understand, don't you? I can't write propaganda."

"Please, please, please, Joe. Just to write on whole very positive image of President; how a great man he is."

Again I look over the letter in my hands. It is addressed to "My dear friend," and is signed "Eddie Bell": the executive chairman and publisher of HarperCollins UK. More troubling than the content is its language. Typed on plain, non-letterhead stationery, with exceptionally rudimentary and clumsy English, it cannot possibly have come from a major publishing house. I feel queasy – and stupid. What other author would not have asked to see the publishing contract first?

"I knew this was going to happen," I confess to Jakov. In the six months we have worked together I have grown to like him. "There's just no way I can do this, even under a pseudonym. Not after I interviewed all those people. They put their confidence in me."

More begging, until I agree to look over the notes in the manuscript and get back to him. After I squeeze a few thousand more bucks out of him, of course. At least I learned something in the Balkans.

Alone, I look over the letter once more. It reads as though it had been translated from Croatian. That day Eddie Bell is in the news as one of Rupert Murdoch's henchmen who killed Chris Patton's book on China because its critical appraisal of China's policies threatened Murdoch's business interests there. But even a politically motivated publisher would never affix his name to: "We have thought up a new a [sic] slogan: Tudjman, an Enigma or Lie and Truth in the World of Politics." That just zings, doesn't it?

The comments in the manuscript are another laugh-riot. In the margins, with a large blue marker, next to the section where I report on the suspected assistance the Croatian military had received from the US, someone has written: "Give me a break!" Proofreading has become so creative these days.

Oh yes, and all of the sections on war crimes have been deleted.

I call Random House and speak with Eddie Bell's assistants. No one there recognizes the name Jakov – or Tudjman.

Over the next week I offer Jakov two options: let me publish the book on my own, or pay me to keep it off the market. I never hear from him again.

* * *

I once thought of returning to Zagreb, with its petit bourgeois shops, first-run American movies, and Jadranka's sweet uncertain smile; and to Sarajevo, with its rows of trinket stores, endless café nights, and Aida's hopeful eyes. But I remain in New York, with questions: What is a writer's obligation to history? Whose history? If history is written by the victors, who speaks for the vanquished – and in whose voice?

Shortly after Tudjman's death, I send the information and interviews I recorded to the War Crimes Tribunal at The Hague. I can no longer in good conscience hide the identity of certain anonymous sources. At this point, I feel, it is time for me to come out from the cold.

* * *

Predrag, a tall, 26-year-old Croatian businessman meets me in my New York apartment to relate a story. Predrag's closest friends were fighting for Croatia during the war, and one night, after many shots of plum brandy, they took their long-haired, smiling buddy down to Gospic, a depressed town just a few kilometers from the Adriatic, at one time home to thousands of ethnic Serbs.

Even though Predrag came from a mixed marriage, his Croat buddies recruited him as one of their own, handed him an automatic rifle, and placed him on the front line. The fighting against the Serbs was sporadic but fierce; several atrocities were carried out by the Croatian paramilitary, including the killing and torture of civilians.

"At noon, every day," recalls Predrag, "there would be one-hour ceasefire, and both armies would meet in the middle of the field to trade food, drink, and cigarettes. One hour later, the fighting and shooting started again." These were people who lived and raised families together, and married each other. Predrag was able to leave Gospic after several weeks, and then, like a few other fortunates, Croatia itself.

Those who remain, with the exception of privileged government employees, are looking to leave.

Through my encounter with Tudjman's fearful Croatia and the sorrowful streets of Sarajevo; from my foolish attempts at international reportage; out of my tortured rescue fantasies to bring the Balkan women home with me, certain patterns come into focus: my growing sense of powerlessness, the implacable nature of territorial politics, and the thin thread that separates us from similar barbarity.

Would I have taken up arms and fought my neighbors if my home was being threatened like those of the residents of Croatia? Would I have fought alongside war criminals, called them heroes; protected them with all my will, if my family was under siege for three or more years? Would I have spoken out against those criminal-heroes, risked jail or worse from a regime schooled in communist-flavored repression? Can anyone judge who has not lived in similar conditions?

In December of '99, Tudjman dies of stomach cancer, escaping The Hague; unlike his fellow Balkan leader Slobodan Milosevic, who every day wrote his autobiography on the stand, until his own death in 2006.

Do I have sympathy for Franjo: sympathy for challenging the Yugoslav communist regime, and for suffering through persecution and jail; sympathy for enduring the lies and propaganda that made him out to be as evil as Hitler; sympathy for his military and political savvy that pushed back Serb aggression, and sealed a lasting peace? Empathy, perhaps – if only he had quit while he was ahead. Before dismantling civil liberties, curtailing freedom of the press and speech, before his complicity in the torture, rape, forced deportation, and murder of innocent civilians.

To be realistic, that would be asking too much. This is, after all, politics.

Lastly, I find more sympathy for him than for myself.

I watch Tudjman's death within the borders of my own privilege, where American foreign policy habitually resembles nothing more than the wanderlust of an aging womanizer; where I contemplate my next journalistic encounter, trusting it might answer a few more questions, but not counting on it.

Chapter Sixteen

"A Yellow Farewell"

> "Even Napoleon had his Watergate."
> **– Yogi Berra**

In the decade following my Balkanization, I learn a few more things.

Like so many of the claims, conspiracies, and dark stories of political dealings and betrayals in the Balkans, the Priest's documents never appear, despite the many lovely smoke-filled hours I spent listening to what a nice man the Mobster was.

In 2000, when Stipe Mesic, one of Tudjman's rivals and the newly elected president of Croatia, took office, a large stash of audio tapes were discovered. They revealed conversations Tudjman had with his aides that disclosed his direct knowledge and cover-up of Croatian war crimes. "If it hadn't been for such men," he was heard to say about the perpetrators, "we wouldn't have Croatia."

The Priest is back in Zagreb, working in the financial industry, where many public leaders go when they want to retire – or hide. He names his company after the Greek goddess of glory and good repute.

George most likely actually freelanced for the CIA. I am not able to prove it, but the pieces fit together too nicely. He now lends his support to the Croatian-American Association.

Before his death, Tudjman signed rights to build a power station in Croatia to Enron, in the hopes of speeding Croatia's entrance into the WTO through Enron's political connections, and help prevent him from being called to The Hague.

Dr. Tony saved the life of Jakov's daughter, and this was the real reason I was hired. (During the dotcom era, Dr. Tony was once slated to run my new Internet company, but sued me when the deal went sour. Enron was also a partner.)

Miles is now a banker in Vienna. He is also the author of a book: *Who Saved Bosnia*. Guess whose picture is on the cover!

In January 2009, Jakov announces production of a new film, to be directed by his son, featuring Armand Assante and Britney Spears. The film is never made.

On April 7, 2010, Croatia's new President Ivo Josipovic formally apologizes for Croatia's role in the Bosnian wars.

In May 2013, the International Criminal Tribunal for the former Yugoslavia found that Tudjman took part in the war crimes against the non-Croat population of Bosnia and Herzegovina.

On July 1, 2013, Croatia becomes the newest member state of the European Union.

In March of 2016, Croatia's justice minister put forth a motion to the Hague war crimes tribunal in an effort to prove Tudjman's innocence. No word on whether my book will be submitted into evidence.

Contrary to rumors, I do not take another paid writing assignment. I don't care how lovely are the lotus blossoms of North Korea.

* * *

For the first time in a thousand years Croatia has independence, at a time when it's fighting its Ustasha past, and the pressure from the West, which wants it to live up to the Dayton Peace Accord, with all of that agreement's negotiated contradictions: the ethnic coalition within ethnic partitioning, the demilitarization amidst the American-backed arming of the Bosnians, the international support of democratic candidates – even when they're not as popular with the locals as the hardline nationalists who defended their homes. War criminals to us; war heroes to them. Pax Americana, and occupation by NATO for a long, long time.

Is that the way Jadranka and Aida thought of me: an occupying foreigner?

Or was I just their ticket out?

I enter the large, glass-enclosed office of Richard Holbrooke. He is at his desk, surrounded by various memorabilia like a curator at the Met.

I meet him when he is vice chairman of Credit Suisse First Boston, before his nomination as the chief American delegate to the UN. He always makes himself available to the media. I pretend I'm one of them.

Before I even sit, he asks, "Who else did you interview for your book?"

"Warren Zimmermann, Herb Okun, Peter Galbraith—"

"Did Galbraith take credit for the Erdut Agreement? He can't, because that was mine."

Did I mention his ego?

Feeling as though I'd never left the Balkans, I assure him I'll set the record straight.

"Now you can't quote me for as long as he's alive, but Tudjman has never, ever lived up to a single agreement about Bosnia. His fixation on the Muslims is borderline psychotic – no, it *is* psychotic. Tudjman's idea of a Muslim fundamentalist front encroaching on the West through the Balkans is nonsense."

Three years later I'm standing on Sixth Avenue in downtown Manhattan, staring at the smoke pouring out of the World Trade Towers, thinking: It's come here. I recall the Priest's words about the fundamentalist Islamic threat in Bosnia that Tudjman always warned about: "*We* will make them fundamentalist, with our behavior," said the Priest. "*We* will make them a threat. That's what will happen."

I meet Holbrooke again in 2005, at New York's New School symposium on a 10-year post-Dayton postmortem. On the panel, Holbrooke ticks off his top four mistakes of the Dayton Agreement:

1) Allowing three armies to exist in a single country

2) Not putting enough power in the central government

3) No Truth and Reconciliation Commission (Says Holbrooke: "Had I seen the movies about [Desmond Tutu's] commission, I would have put it in the Agreement.")

4) Calling Republic Srpska 'Republic Srpska' (How about "The No-Shave Zone"?)

"I guess I'm supposed to be the voice of gloom," says Chuck Sudetic in his turn. An American Croat, Sudetic covered the war in Bosnia for *The New York Times*. Now at the war crimes tribunal in The Hague, he speaks of the "mother lode of transcripts" from the Croatian government that show how decisions made by President Tudjman created a whiplash effect, resulting in several atrocities in Bosnia committed by Croatians.

After the panel, I ask Sudetic: "Had Tudjman lived, would he have been called to The Hague?" He pauses, sizing me up, and says: "I can assure you that he would."

I have the opportunity for just two more questions: Is the Priest still alive, and if so would he soon be called to The Hague?

He looks me up and down, his face saying, "Who the fuck are you?"

"He's alive," he finally replies, starting to back away from me, "and I can't comment."

To this day, despite the pressures, entreaties, and outright bribes from various parties, I keep my promise to the Priest not to reveal his name to the world as Vlado Pogarcic. After all, I'm a professional journalist, right?

My exchange with journalist Laura Silber is almost as brief. I ask her about George, my Virgil and literary poltergeist.

"Oh yes, the little war criminal," she jokingly responds.

"Rumor has it he was CIA, or worked for the CIA," I say.

"I would not be surprised," she laughs, "but I really don't know."

During the panel there are the anticipated parallels with Iraq, the delving into the minutiae of whether Banja Luka should have been taken by the Croat-Muslim army during the war, and a few nods to Darfur.

But the evening is best summed up by my final fleeting encounter with Holbrooke, whom I ambush as he enters the building.

"I'm Joe Tripician," I begin my run-on sentence, "we met in '98, when I interviewed you for my book on Tudjman, which was never published because the Croatian government didn't like what I wrote."

He shakes my hand, smiles wanly, and then marches ahead, saying, "I'm looking for the men's room."

Chapter Seventeen

"Balkan Hangover"

> "Truth is always the enemy of power.
> And power the enemy of truth."
> **– Edward Abbey**

At nights when I can sleep, the fevered dreams take hold. In one, it is Aida, and she is crying: "I heard of you Americans who panic when your TV breaks, who scream when your coffee is cold, who cry when your lover leaves you. I will never understand it. This cannot be what comes from democracy and civil society. Let me know; please tell me, Joe, it is not true. I would rather face all the guns from this war, than a life of slavery to such banality."

In another, it is Mate Boban, presiding over his nationalist comrades in a rambling, rundown shack carved deep into the mountains. He tells me he is simply misunderstood, and reminds me of the horrors my own America inflicted upon the Native Americans, the blacks, the Mexicans, the Japanese, the Vietnamese, the Iraqis, etc.

"How can you call *us* criminals, when you have the death penalty and our country doesn't? You set the terms because you are the only superpower left in the world. But do not think for a moment you will have us fooled. We know your game. And we know your weakness. You will never stoop to getting your feet dirty in our country because we can stop you. And all we have to do is send a few of your precious American troops home in bags of bodies, and you will run away, leaving this land, finally, to our people who will reclaim it as their rightful, ancient heritage."

"You don't believe that historical, nationalist speech, do you?" I ask, weary of it all.

"It's worked so far," he admits, with some satisfaction.

There is a contradictory theme which runs through Croatian conversations: the idea that the West (and specifically the United States) bears significant responsibility for not preventing, through military intervention, the war in the former Yugoslavia, and hence it now becomes morally obligated to economically and politically assist Croatia, one of the first victims in the war; conversely, the thinking goes, the newly formed nation of Croatia has a right to self-determination and should not be obliged to bend to the West's (and specifically the United States') will in matters political.

This is the Balkan Hangover: the combination of seeking succor from the West and acceptance into the international community, with all the attendant military and financial support, is constantly played against the new drive for independence, the resentment of having one's peccadilloes spoken about in public, and the defensiveness against being accused of any wrong.

"My sense of history is that there's eventually either justice or revenge," reflects Michael Sells, current Professor of Islamic History and Literature at the Divinity School of the University of Chicago. "By that I mean not perfect justice, but at least some gesture toward justice. And that's another reason why enforcing what's good about the Dayton Accords is important, and supporting the War Crimes Tribunal. If the indicted war criminals are actually tried and people see that at least some small group of people has been held accountable, that's an important symbol. And it's certainly one of the things that Serbs never forgot about World War II: that most of the Ustasha got away scot-free. And the Serb nationalists kept that desire for revenge for 50 years, while smiling at their Croatian neighbors and drinking with them and going to parties with them and marrying them."

Chapter Eighteen

"How Do I Put This in My Resume?"

*"If you can't get rid of the skeleton in your closet,
you'd best teach it to dance."*
– George Bernard Shaw

I write several versions of this small story, each one with an alternate ending. That's the problem with memoirs, they don't end like they do in the movies; they just stop, like life, unfinished and unformed and messy.

    Here's one ending:

    …I wave goodbye to the two sweetest creatures in Sarajevo and start to board the plane, when, suddenly, three thugs grab me and rudely escort me to an empty windowless waiting room. Then I'm blindfolded and dumped in the back of some van. No one is speaking English. I'm going to die, and I won't even know who or why.

    We drive for hours. When we stop, I'm hauled outside, and my blindfold is taken off. I'm in a small abandoned factory in the middle of the woods, surrounded by arid rocks and intractable mountains, and dozens of armed guards; none of them too friendly.

I'm brought upstairs to a large office; the only light comes from the broken windows. Behind the oak desk sits a grey-suited man with slicked-back silver hair. He looks like a banker, but he's the spitting image of the Mobster. Several lines have aged his face as he greets me very cordially, offering me a cigarette.

"No, thanks."

Then he holds up a stack of papers.

The Mobster speaks, pretending he's my closest friend, "I have read your book."

"How did you get that?"

"The question for today is: why are there two?"

"I don't—"

"Before you answer, let me give you my critical review. In first book, you write a character called 'the Mobster'—" he laughs "—who killed innocent Muslims. Tsk, tsk. In second book, you praise this man by his real name, Mate Boban, as noble leader who saved Croat and Muslim people. Which author are you? Because I like author of Book Two much better."

He nods to one of the guards, who pulls out a pistol and presses it against my head.

"Do you know why you were hired?"

Another nod; and the guard cocks the gun.

"Do you know why you were hired?"

"Of course. I've done a good job so far, haven't I? I mean, I've done a better job serving the mission than being just a loyal soldier."

Now I have his attention.

"I was hired to rehabilitate Tudjman's image, and help keep him out of The Hague. That was the soldier's job. Our mission, however, is to present a fair and accurate portrait of your President, your country, and your cause. And we couldn't exactly do that and tip off the government in Zagreb, now could we?

"That's why we wrote two books: one for the President to see, the other for the public to read. The second book is the one we plan to publish.

"You served the cause better than your President, who had to blame you for political reasons. You took the fall, so that your people could be victorious."

He takes this in, but he's not pleased. "You tell me why Mate Boban was noble savior of his people."

"You armed the Croats in Bosnia to protect the Croatian coast. You formed Herzeg-Bosna – 'Greater Croatia'– to reclaim Bosnia back into Croatia. But most important, you kept the Serbs and the Muslims from overrunning the country. You did America's dirty work for us, and not many know that."

He relaxes ever so slightly, never letting down his guard. "As you say in America: so far, so good. You Americans keep your eyes on the Muslims. They will cause you a lot of suffering, if you are not eternally vigilant."

I pray I've escaped the bullet.

"One more question: who are this 'we' you talk of? You are not sole author?"

"I am the author, but with much assistance from my associate – George Rudman."

"Georgie! Oh, why did you not say so?"

He nods to the guard, who releases me and puts away his pistol.

"And here I thought that idiot Jakov was behind this, when all along it was our friends from CIA! How wonderful! Now that I hear your plan, it is, I must say, delightfully deceptive. Please to have drink with us!"

I drink so much that night, but stay sober, till the moment I am delivered back to the Holiday Inn Sarajevo.

I meet Aida and her boy in the back of a mosque and tell her what I pieced together before my meeting with the Mobster: that Jadranka informed the American Embassy about my meeting with the Priest, finally landing her a job.

But only when the gunmetal presses against my temple do I realize that George took my manuscript and edited it into Book Two – the rehabilitation of the Mobster. Why, you ask? Another thank-you gift from the CIA, who appreciated the ethnic cleansing the Mobster did in Bosnia. Their biggest thank-you gift, however, was staging the Mobster's death. That's one way to escape The Hague.

We leave the mosque, and before we're off the block what must be the only limousine in Sarajevo pulls up. Douglas Davidson flies out, surrounded by three bodyguards, and welcomes us royally into the limo.

"Hello, Doug. What brings you to Sarajevo?"

"You'll forgive me if we forgo the formalities. This car can either take you to the airport, or to the local prison. I recommend the airport; the food at the prison is just a notch below."

I have nothing to give you, Davidson. My laptop and papers were stolen from my hotel room. You see, I spent last night away, and couldn't tip the maid—"

"Mr. Tripician—"

"—and they short-sheeted me, and—"

"Just hand us the Priest's documents, and you fly back to New York."

"Aida and her son get visas, and tickets to fly with me."

She screams, "No, Joe, Please—!"

He doesn't wait to signal his guards, who search me and retrieve the Priest's envelope from my pocket.

"See how much easier it is when you cooperate?"

On the flight to Vienna, Aida is despondent.

"Why so glum, sugar? You got your freedom, and you got me."

She turns to me and lets it out. "Why is it so easy for you? Is it because you never experienced war that you do not have this hunger for justice? Or for revenge? People who do not receive justice seek revenge. That is why even our Muslim people seek revenge, because they cannot find justice.

"Do not you hunger for justice, American writer? To tell your story to The Hague?"

"Oh, that's our next stop, after Vienna. And I brought the Priest's papers, too." I pull a white envelope from my back pocket.

"But you gave papers to American Embassy man."

"That's the advantage of Photoshop and a good printer. I still have the originals."

"And what did you give him?"

"A silly little book about alien abductions – something I've become an expert on."

Forgive me, dear reader, but if I can't be the hero in my own story, what benefit is it to be a writer?

* * *

The final words I'll leave to a real Balkan hero. Vesna Terselic is a peace activist who founded the Anti-War Campaign of Croatia. In 1998, she was a joint recipient of the Right Livelihood Award, along with Katarina Kruhonja of the Centre for Peace, Non-violence and Human Rights.

She speaks softly, but with absolute assurance, and transparent humility. "Milosovic, Tudjman, Izetbegovic, and the International Community all carry a big responsibility for what happened in this war. They had a lot of power. And that huge chunk of responsibility is clearly connected with that chunk of power.

"Each of us has our own piece of responsibility. Not of guilt. Guilt is absolutely for the ones who committed the crimes. That's very clear. The crime has a name. The person who did it has a name. But the responsibility is entirely another issue. And each of us has a part of the responsibility, which is connected with the amount of power we have. And each of us has some power. Maybe it's a small amount, but it is some power."

ADDENDUM 1

"What Could Go Wrong?"

AGREEMENT

This Agreement made as of July 25, 1997, between Jakov Sedlar / The Croatian Embassy ("Purchaser") at 369 Lexington Ave., New York, NY 10017 and Joe Tripician c/o CoDirections, Inc., at 560 West 43rd Street Suite #8K, New York, NY 10036 ("Author").

WHEREAS, Purchaser desires to have a work, part biography and part interview written about President Franjo Tudjman (hereinafter referred to as the "Work"); and Purchaser and Author desire to have the Work published; the parties hereto agree as follows:

1. Author shall write the Work and Purchaser shall provide Author with any such data, access and information as may be required to write the Work. Purchaser shall grant Author access to pertinent documents, where available and will use its best efforts to secure interviews with President Tudjman, and President Tudjman's former and present colleagues and aides, for a length, time, and place to be mutually determined.

2. Author shall write the Work on a nonexclusive basis.

3. Author shall have creative control and Author shall deliver to the Purchaser on or before December 1, 1997, one copy of the manuscript of the Work. Author shall not be responsible for delays caused by any wars, civil riots, strikes, fires, Governmental restrictions, material shortages, or other similar or dissimilar circumstances beyond his control, and in the event of the occurrence of any such circumstance the delivery date shall be deemed extended until the next Spring or Fall season immediately succeeding the removal of such delay.

4. Author hereby grants to Purchaser, during the full term of the copyright of the Work, the sole and exclusive Right to publish and sell the Work in book form, and to license others to do so.

5. All copyrights, renewals, and extensions thereof, in and to the material contained in the Work, shall be secured by Author and held in his name, as the sole and exclusive author and proprietor thereof, and the characters and characterizations therein, in all languages, forms, and media now or hereafter known. The foregoing shall include all literary rights, copyrights, and all intangible property rights of any kind or nature in any written or oral material prepared for or by, or made available to, Author in connection with the Work and all intangible property rights in any taperecording made pursuant thereto. Any materials used in connection with the Work that are not incorporated into the Work shall be the sole property of the Purchaser.

6. The Purchaser shall, within one year from the date on which the Work is camera ready for the press, publish, or cause to be published, the Work, at Purchaser's own expense. If Purchaser does not publish or cause to be published the Work within one year of the date of delivery, then all rights shall revert to the Author and this Agreement shall terminate.

7. Nothing in this Agreement shall cause Author, at any time, to return payments already due according to the payment schedule in Paragraph 8 below.

8. In consideration of the Right granted herein, Purchaser shall pay Author in the following manner:

a. ADVANCE: Purchaser shall pay Author the guaranteed sum of forty thousand ($40,000) United States dollars to be paid according to the following schedule. (i) $30,000 no later than July 29, 1997. (ii) $10,000 upon delivery of the final manuscript.

b. ROYALTIES: Purchaser shall pay or cause the Publisher to pay Author the nonrecoupable sum of 15% of the retail price for every copy of the Work sold.

All payments are to be wire transferred to Joe Tripician, c/o CoDirections, Inc. to the following account:
Chase Manhattan Bank
1501 Broadway
New York, New York 10022
Account#: ...
Routing#: ...

9. The Purchaser will provide the Author with semiannual statements of sales of the Work and receipts as of June 30 and December 1 of each year and will forward such statements, with remittances in accordance with this Agreement, within three months after those dates. If subsequent to one year from the publication date, no earnings have been payable to the Author hereunder during two consecutive accounting periods, then and in such event, the Author may demand in writing at any time thereafter the reassignment to himself of all rights granted to the Purchaser. If the Author shall make any such demand, the Purchaser has six months during which to make arrangements; for reprinting or other use of the Work or may submit other evidence of anticipated earnings from the Work, and upon the submission of satisfactory evidence of to such effect this Agreement shall continue in full force and effect as if no such demand had been made; but if at the expiration of such six months period the Purchaser shall not have made any such arrangement or submitted such evidence, all rights revert to the Author.

10. The sole authorship credit for the Work on the cover, jacket, title page, and any other place where authorship credit is customarily included on a book, in any and all media, and on advertising and promotion in which the Work is used or licensed shall be as follows: "Written by Joe Tripician"; however, Purchaser agrees that Author shall have the right to use a pseudonym or withhold use of his name if Author so desires. This provision applies to all editions of the Work published by any publisher and to all editions of the Work or portions of the Work licensed for publication by any publisher and any license or purchaser of any of the subsidiary rights.

11. Purchaser warrants that it is free to enter into this Agreement, and that insofar as material created or supplied by Purchaser is concerned, Purchaser warrants that this material is original, that it does not contain any libelous or unlawful matter, and that it does not invade any right to privacy nor infringe any statutory or common law copyright. Purchaser agrees to hold Author harmless from any and against all claims of libel or of copyright infringement or of invasion of privacy or similar rights arising out of material created by Purchaser in the Work.

12. This Agreement shall be governed and interpreted as a contract negotiated and executed under the laws of the State of New York. The parties hereto hereby consent to the jurisdiction of the Supreme Court of New York State, County of New York for any disputes arising out of this Agreement.

13. This Agreement shall be binding and shall inure to the benefit of the heirs and personal representatives of the Author and the successors and assigns of the Purchaser. The Purchaser may not assign this Agreement without prior written consent of the Author.

14. This Agreement contains the complete understanding of the parties hereto, and no modification or waiver of any provision hereof shall be valid unless in writing signed by the parties.

IN WITNESS WHEREOF, the parties have executed this Agreement as of the date first above written.

AGREED AND ACCEPTED
[SIGNED: JAKOV SEDLAR]
By: [SIGNED: CROATIAN CONSULATE]
Its: [SIGNED: COUNSEL]
AGREED AND ACCEPTED
[SIGNED: JOE TRIPICIAN]
Date: [SIGNED: 7/28/97]

Addendum 2

"Love Letter from Miles"

Translated from Croatian:

PERMANENT MISSION OF THE REPUBLIC OF CROATIA TO THE UNITED NATIONS

[Mission address; coat of arms, etc.]

Date: December 29, 1997

TOP SECRET

Deliver to:

Office of the President, Franjo Tudjman

Foreign Ministry, Mate Granic

Delivered by:

Miomir Zuzul, ambassador to US

Jakov Sedlar, cultural attaché, NYC

[NOTE about obtaining the first part of the manuscript of the book by Joe Tripician about the President of Republic of Croatia.]

From a confidential source inside the Random House publishing house, special counsel Miles Raguz obtained the first draft of the already finished manuscript of the book about the President of the Republic of Croatia written by Joe Tripician. Enclosed are the excerpts from the manuscript and their short analysis. The entire 137 pages manuscript we are sending by diplomatic mail. Source seeks anonymity, so we ask for discretion in handling of this matter.

Compiled by:

Vitomir Miles Raguz

Special Advisor

[signed by] General Consul Ivan Simunovic

TOP SECRET

ANALYSIS of the first part of the manuscript of the book by Joe Tripician about the President of the Republic of Croatia

Summary: The book reflects the negative perceptions of the President, Republic of Croatia and Herceg-Bosna. It mentions all the criticism of the Western public opinion against the President, yet it does not place it in the necessary context, i.e., it does not explain local circumstances unrecognizable to the Western public. The writer hints that the President might be connected with the murders of Blaz Kraljevic and Ante Paradzik. Manuscript appears as if the history of conflict was 'copied' from the pages of The New York Times. The rare author's independent conclusions are, also, anti-Croat. For example, author states on page 83: "If we say that Serbs returned ethnic cleansing to life, then we can say that Croats perfected it."

The manuscript is full of, to the international community already well-known, negative perceptions about the President, Republic of Croatia, Herceg-Bosna and the history of Croatia. We are highlighting the following comments:

1. History of conflict was presented using the known logic of the media disinclined to the Croatian cause (crude nationalism, equalizing the responsibility of Belgrade and Zagreb, presenting Muslims as the only victims, etc.). Given that the author is not an expert in history, nor is he well informed about the most recent conflict, it appears that for his background information he most likely uses the articles published in *The New York Times*. Croatian identity is presented as "nationalism," which as an idea is unacceptable to the Western reader.

2. Current conflict in the draft version of this book is related to the events from NDH (Independent State of Croatia). Serbs are presented as a majority in the anti-fascist movement, and Chetnicks as yet another anti-fascist group. Muslims are historically innocent group that joined Partisans during the WWII. The draft is overburdened with the paradigm of Ustasha: Serbs feared new Ustashas; Tudjman partially adopted Ustasha ideology; Tudjman was supported politically and financially by Ustasha émigrés; Hercegovci are still Ustashas today; Serbs did to Muslims in this conflict the same that Croats did to Serbs during the NDH; there is a historic alliance between Croatia and Germany.

3. Politics of R.Croatia towards Bosnia & Hercegovina is explained exclusively within the context of extreme nationalism and territorial pretensions, and as such put to blame. The agreement between Milosevic and Tudjman about the division of Bosnia is highlighted on several occasions. The role of Croats and Serbs in B&H is equalized. The crimes of Serbs and Croats in the R. of C. are equalized. The author picks Borovo Selo and the murder of Reichel-Kier as the pivotal events for the beginning of war in the R. of C.

4. The author nearly exclusively quotes those Western writers that are reserved about Croatia, or even openly anti-Croat, like Richard West, Warren Zimmerman, Laura Silber and Robert Donia. Also, he often quotes Ivo Banac and the person that he calls "The Priest." The author quotes Slvaneka Drakulic, too – and she is known to have accused Croatian identity as an unacceptable nationalism. He quotes Lojze Peterle and Herbert Okun in positive light for the President.

5. The author firmly puts R. of C. on the Balkans and assigns all the negative events in the region to the "Balkan" way of life, behavior or conducting of warfare.

6. From the manuscript we take a couple of quotes, translated to Croatian:

– If Franjo's early identification with Ustashas (p. 5)

– Checkerboard – Croatian checkered coat of arms even today evokes horror in the hearts of WWII survivors (p. 7)

– Ustasha reign of terror is virtually unparalleled in modern history (p. 12)

– Stepinac, the archbishop of Zagreb, supported Ustashas and blessed Pavelic (p. 13)

– Tudjman's figures [about the Jasenovac victims] lead to wrong conclusions (p. 14)

– This proposal to de-Serbianize Croatian language now looks ridiculous and divisive (p.39)

– The difference was that Croatian liberals saw the injustice, but also a danger in the declaration of independence without addressing and finding a solution for the worries and fears of the Serb minority. The white socks did not care about that at all. (p. 57)

– As one Hercegovac explained: "Here only three things grow: snakes, rocks and Ustasha." (p. 58)

– Their laughter provoked him to utter the words now known as his greatest 'faux pas,' albeit just one of the many to follow. (p. 60)

– However, the propaganda in Croatian media was equally as fierce (p. 60)

– Although Serbs were the majority in Knin, the region was controlled by Croatia … (p.61)

– [This goal for Tudjman] had included all ornaments: checkerboard, nationalist songs, honor guard to rival Tito's, and the renaming of streets in Zagreb from Partisan to NDH names. (p. 63)

– The new nationalist government took a direct control over radio, television and principal print media, to prepare them, as the official explanation asserted, for the transition to the market economy. The direct consequence was that the HDZ controlled the opposition vote. In the schoolbooks all stories about the Partisans and the anti-fascist movement were deleted, and state employees – from mailmen to social workers – were required to sign the loyalty oath. (p. 64)

– Fear and hate, imported by extremists on both sides... (p. 73)

– If we say that Serbs returned ethnic cleansing to life, then we can say that Croats perfected it. (p. 83)

– In other words, Franjo made a scapegoat out of Vukovar. (p. 85)

– Cruelty of the Serbs [B&H] rushed through the villages and townships. Their methods were the same as those of Ustashas in 1941 (p. 91)

– Mistrust and suspicion will quickly break down feeble Croatian-Muslim alliance and result in the bloodiest episode in this bloody, little war. (p. 92)

– As are the Bosnian Serbs, ... as are the Bosnian Croats ... (p. 95)

– In fact, he [Tudjman] hated Muslims. Looked upon them as inferiors ... (p.97)

– Muslims found themselves squeezed between Serbs on the East and Croats on the West. Massacres that followed were the bloodiest since the WWII. It was a slaughterhouse. It was genocide. And everything was allowed. (p.105)

– Croatian Guard brigades occupied Western Hercegovina. (p. 103)

– Both Serbs and Croats blocked food delivery to Bosnians (p. 104)

– Majority [of POW's in B&H] were held by Bosnian Croats (p. 112)

– I have an impression that by the end of the 1993 he [Tudjman] listened more to me [Galbraith] than to his advisors. (p. 114)

– While Granic discussed with international representatives building of

Muslim-Croatian alliance, Bosnian Croat delegates coordinated their military attacks on Muslims with the Croatian secretary of defense, Gojko Susak, loyal to Tudjman. (p. 122)

– True, Tudjman in fact did not care that much about Bosnian Croats (p. 126)

– In July, Tudjman's army took two towns in Western Bosnia (p. 131)

– During 'The Storm,' Croatian soldiers looted and burned more than 20,000 Serbian homes. (p. 133)

Comment:

Author's motivation for such a negative approach perhaps comes out of market reasoning. Western markets buy/sell certain concepts, and R. of C. already has an image that belongs into marketable negative concepts.

Compiled by:

V.M. Raguz

Special advisor

ADDENDUM 3

"AKA Eddie Bell"

[No letterhead, no return address, no to address]

My Dear Friend,

I have just finished reading the biography of the Croatian President Tudjman. I have also received commentaries from two of my sources who have also read it. Thus, I would like to ask you for several things which could put this book on the world market and make it more commercial.

It is in my opinion, and that of my colleagues, that Croatia has been one-sidedly misrepresented in the media. It is because of this fact that we want to see fair profiles done on Croatia and its president, President Tudjman. We would like to publish the above mentioned biography as well as two other books on Croatia.

I feel that we have to stay away from any comparison between Tito and Tudjman since it can damage the commercial success of the book.

Also, it is absolutely untrue that Tudjman, [type blacked out] from being a communist figure became a fascist supporter.

Tudjman, in my eyes, is not someone who wants to divide Bosnia and Herzegovina; my assistants agree. This point is extremely important – not only because it is the truth but also because it can hurt us commercially. This delicate issue has to be dealt with decisively because many of the US journalists are avid supporters of this belief. What has to be emphasized is the fact that Tudjman saved many Muslims from genocide.

It is important to strip Tudjman of his unflattering image as a dictator. If this were true neither me nor my company would embark on this project.

Mr. Tripician has made a formidable thing, but please ask him to adjust few [sic] more details which will help us to better promote the book. We have thought up a new a [sic] slogan: Tudjman, an Enigma or Lie and Truth in the World of Politics. I truly loved the movie that you and Tripician have done. Lets [sic] make the ending of the book as if it were a movie ending: a man who dreamt about creating a state and who eventually succeeded. I want to create a more humane story about a man who created a state in unbelievable circumstances, against all odds, in spite the [sic] "big powers'" wishes.

I think that this will not be a big undertaking for Joe, but it could definitely change the course of events; hopefully it could make it easier on all of us. Also, it is not necessary to repeat that which has been said so many times, and which is basically not true.

Please, call me as soon as possible about the deadline for the scrip [sic] since everything is ready regarding the publishing of the biography.

All the best,

[signed]

Eddie Bell

General Manager

London, February 2, 1998

ADDENDUM 4

"Biting My Tongue"

[Return address]

March 10, 1998

Jakov Sedlar

Croatian Consulate

369 Lexington Avenue

11th Floor

New York, NY 10017

Dear Jakov,

I have been struggling to resolve a dilemma, admittedly one mostly of my own making. Before I address that dilemma, let me first respond to the written comments on my book:

I too believe that, on the whole, Croatia has been one-sidedly represented in the Western media. That is one reason why a fair and accurate portrait of Franjo Tudjman is needed. I also believe, however, that if I were to incorporate the changes suggested by you, it would only do more damage to the reputation of Tudjman and Croatia, for the simple reason that such changes would render the book just another propaganda mortar in the already overcrowded Balkan propaganda wars.

I sincerely believed our mutual task was to put to rest the myths and lies about Tudjman, but not to skirt any controversy either. Contrary to the letter from "Eddie Bell," controversy only enhances the commercial viability of books.

Specifically, many of the issues mentioned in the letter and within the notes in the manuscript are off base. First, nowhere in my book do I say that Tudjman became a fascist supporter. He was, as I detailed, supported by many hardline émigrés, some of whom had fascist leanings. Second, Tudjman has always used the 1939 Croatian map as his ideal. This is irrefutable. As I wrote, his designs on Western Herzegovina were not only for security purposes to protect Dalmatia and prevent Croatia from being cut in half during the war, but also to create an ethnically pure statelet dependent on Zagreb. This also is irrefutable.

Finally, I do not believe the book paints Tudjman as a dictator. As we both know, he is a military general whose style befits a bygone era, and whose autocratic tendencies have caused great trouble for Croatia in the eyes of the West.

Nevertheless, I still believe that to totally expunge these elements from the book would do both Tudjman and Croatia a huge disservice; it would neuter the arguments and leave the book completely devoid of credibility. Wouldn't you rather have the Western media say, "Maybe we were wrong about this country: look how forthcoming it is about its own president"?

As you recall from our very first discussions, and as written in my contract, I retain the creative control of the book. That does not mean I am unwilling to listen to comments. I welcome the opportunity to discuss the book with any representative from the publisher.

Now to my dilemma: Another reason I am reluctant to make the suggested changes in the book is the damage it would do to my own name and professional reputation. If I am seen as just a mouthpiece of the Croatian government, my future writing career would be severely limited indeed. I also realize, however, that I would not be able to make these changes and then release the book under a pseudonym, primarily because every person I interviewed for this book is aware that I am writing it; hence the pseudonym would be a transparent veil. I am particularly concerned about the effect such a book would have on the very important people I interviewed who have placed their confidence in me: Richard Holbrooke, for example. I could also be faced with significant legal ramifications: misrepresentation is just one of them.

So, we are now faced with a limited number of options; but these options are still viable, and with your help and suggestions, they could resolve our mutual dilemma.

One: Since you owe me a final payment of $10,000 on my contract, you could withhold that payment, in effect breaking the contract, which would allow me to publish the manuscript on my own. I would also consider repaying you the initial $40,000 if and when I succeed in placing its publication elsewhere, and if and when I receive said monies from its publication.

Two: You could use the book's structure as a base to write your own biography of the President, providing you do not use any of my interviews, or copy my use of language in the book. This would not preclude you from conducting your own interviews, of course. As a payment for keeping my book off the market, you would then pay me the $10,000 you still owe, plus another $50,000: this would represent the anticipated lost earnings from my book's exploitation in all media and markets.

I'm sure there are other options, if we both are willing to put our heads together and attempt to work this out. I am most concerned that you understand my position, and realize that I am honestly trying to find a workable solution.

Sincerely,

Joe Tripician

Enc: Croatian translation of this letter

About the Author

Joe Tripician is an award-winning Writer/Producer/Director and Playwright. His work has been broadcast across America, Europe and Japan, and has shown at the Cannes Film Festival.

Joe received his first EMMY award for the documentary *Metaphoria* broadcast in the US on PBS in 1991.

In his varied career Joe has worked with such talents as: Jim Henson, Lou Reed, Jeff Buckley, Steve Buscemi, Jim Carroll, Quentin Crisp, Lydia Lunch, TONY award winners Marc Shaiman and Scott Wittman, as well as legendary filmmaker D. A. Pennebaker on the Oscar-nominated film "The War Room."

Joe's humor book, *The Official Alien Abductee's Handbook*, was published by Andrews and McMeel in 1997. Author and Futurist Robert Anton Wilson called it: "The funniest book I've read since the

Warren Report." Famed scientist John C. Lilly said: "Joe Tripician has achieved the impossible: a truly funny book on alien abductions."

In 1996 Joe wrote, recorded and performed an alien hillbilly song ("Ozark Melody") with the legendary Jeff Buckley along with musical partner Frederick Reed.

In May of 2002, Joe performed in his one-man play, *Balkanized at Sunrise*, to a sold-out audience at Dixon Place Theater in New York City. The play was based on his 1997 trip to the Balkans. His Balkan journey began when the Croatian government hired him to write an official biography of their president.

Joe lives in Brazil with his wife and two daughters.

Website: http://joetripician.com